Gripped by the Culture

Canvassing Common Cultural Influences in the Church

Ericka McCrutcheon

Gripped by the Culture
Canvassing Cultural Influences in the Church

Cover Artwork by PJ Robins
TYRO Publishing Services
http://www.tyropublishing.com
For more information please write to:
Attention: Ericka McCrutcheon -erickamcc@sbcglobal.net

Printed in the United States of America
First Printing, 2015
ISBN-13: 978-0692530566
ISBN-10: 0692530568

TYRO Publishing Services

Dedication

I dedicate this book to many people who have influenced my life and gave me a solid foundation to build upon in the Lord Jesus Christ. The late Rev. Mae McCray Brooks, Grandmother, who was a Pentecostal Preacher and a lover of the Word of God and prayer. Eddie Clarence Williams, childhood Pastor, who labored in prayers that helped to chart my course in God. To my father, the late George W. McCray, Sr. and mother, Annie B. McCray, who encouraged me to follow God and to fulfill the calling upon my life. In the middle of this writing, mom transitioned to Heaven (Jan 28, 2012). However, prior to her departure, she encouraged me to finish and not give up sharing this message. To my beloved husband of 26 years and Pastor, Rev. John T. McCrutcheon. Our love grows sweeter each day. Thank you for the many discussions, teachings, and advice and for an awesome life in ministry together. You have been my strength and sounding board. Thanks for recognizing the spiritual warfare and praying for me as I worked to get this book completed. Faith is the victory that overcomes. Much love!

Special Thanks

Bishop James E. McKnight, Presiding Bishop of the Church of God By Faith, Gainesville, FL; Pastor Samuel Jones, Open Door Baptist Church, Gainesville, FL; Ministers Winston and Sandra Bradley, College Outreach Pastors of Agape Faith Center, Gainesville, FL; the late Apostle Ronald Thomas and Marvanelle Thomas (Garvin) (College Pastors), Agape Faith Center, Gainesville, FL; the late Evangelist/Pastor Ruben S. Williams and Eula Williams, Holy Ghost Outreach Ministries, Gainesville, FL; the late Rev. Kenneth E. Hagin, Kenneth Hagin Ministries, Tulsa, OK; Pastors Kenneth W. and Lynette Hagin, Rhema Bible Church, Broken Arrow, OK; the late Pastor Clinton Utterbach and Pastor Sarah Utterbach, Redeeming Love Christian Center, Nanuet, NY; Co-Pastor Theresa Watts, The Rock Church, Tulsa, OK. Pastor Wilford Darden, Jesus is Alpha & Omega Ministries, Houston, TX.

Thank you for being faithful to preach the Gospel that saved me and for your many words of encouragement, correction and training in ministry. I love you and thank you! Thank you! Thank you!

Endorsement

"Gripped by the Culture" is sure to challenge, arrest and engage the runaway pop culture in the Church. Thought provoking and scripturally enlightening, giving insight on the importance of Believers renewing their mind and having a biblical worldview.

Pastor John McCrutcheon

I remember this statement from my youth growing up, "If you do not stand for something, you will fall for anything!" "Gripped by the Culture" will challenge you to stand for something. Whether you agree with the content or disagree with it, the teachings and exposure to Scripture will provoke you to stop and think. It is said that knowledge is power and what you do with the knowledge will determine your destiny. I am honored to write this forward for my best friend and sister in Christ.

Pastor Theresa Watts

When Pastor Ericka McCrutcheon told me she was writing a book on being "Gripped by the Culture", I could hardly keep my composure. If you know her, like I have for the past 22 years, you know she has a powerful word ready to be pushed out and birthed. This book presents experience and research based on the culture which we live in today. It offers a look into the heart of where you live and moves us to either act or fall by the way side.

Pastor Tyrone M. Holloway

Table of Contents

Foreword

This book will help every Believer recognize popular cultural trends that are contrary to Scripture that have become rather acceptable and common in the church. The Bible is the most relevant book of all ages! It is never obsolete, and its truths endure to all generations. Thus it is the trusted source for inspiration from God and is profitable for doctrine, for reproof, for correction, for instruction in righteousness. This book will canvass common cultural influences in the Church and will shine light from the Scriptures for transformation for those who are "Gripped by the Culture."

Introduction

Pastoring more than 20 years, we have witnessed the rise of cavalier attitudes and behaviors from Christians within the Church. The inspiration for this book comes to heart as a critique of the trends and common behaviors that are more and more acceptable to the Body of Christ. This book lends a view in hopes that every Believer will take inventory of their behavior as a member of the Body of Christ. We are admonished, in 2 Corinthians 13:5, to examine and prove ourselves whether we are in the faith. It seems that everything is allowed, and there are no longer any moral constraints. Set apart living is viewed as "ole fashioned" and obsolete. Rather than Believers thinking and behaving biblically, many think and behave according the dictates of popular culture. I am writing about these things because they matter to God because God's word clearly addresses the issues under discussion in this book. We, who are faithful disciples, should give attention to and conform to His revealed will.

This book is not designed to be a tool for legalism or condemnation for any Believer. However, it is written to expose the infiltration of the worldly culture within the Church. Jesus Christ came first to transform lives. Only after the transformation, behavior modification can occur. Transformation comes by being born again of His Spirit, but behavior modification comes by the renewing of the mind. I trust the reader will not dismiss the contents in this book as legalistic meddling. "Gripped by the Culture" is not intended to offend, disgrace or wound anyone who may disagree, but to bring simply to light how contrary cultural beliefs have impacted the thinking of many Christians. Some topics you will read are controversial in today's culture and even in the Church.

Unmanaged Souls

An influential pastor once said that information is not the problem in the Body of Christ but the application and **unmanaged souls**. I tend to agree with this statement. We are admonished in the Word of God to put on the new man and be renewed in the spirit of our minds. Consider this passage of scripture.

Eph 4:21-24 KJV

21 If so be that ye have heard him and have been taught by him, as the truth is in Jesus:

22 That ye put off concerning the former conversation the old man, which is corrupt according to the deceitful lusts;

23 And be renewed in the spirit of your mind;

24 And that ye put on the new man, which after God is created in righteousness and true holiness.

Every Believer has the responsibility for renewing their mind with the Word of God. **God is not going to do this for us**. Renewing the mind is the Believer's responsibility! By learning this truth and conforming to it, putting it to work in life, a measure of grace is imparted which impacts behavior. Renewing the mind frees the Believer from the ideas, trends, norms, ways and behaviors of the world's popular culture. The world becomes less appealing when the Word of God enlightens the mind. Jesus intended for The Church (the called out one's) to influence the culture; not the culture to influence the Church. The world is to see a different spirit and behavior about the Church. The born again life comes that we may know God and experience His way of doing things. It is to involve our thoughts, behaviors and lives in every area so to infect and affect the culture in which we live. God has already given the Church everything that it needs to be victorious over the world and worldliness. Believers are not afraid of the world neither worldliness because we have the power to overcome it.

1 John 5:4 says, *"for whatsoever is born of God overcometh the world: and this is the victory that overcometh the world, even our faith." KJV*

Every believer should have this passage of Scripture hidden in their heart, saturated in their mind and confessed daily from their lips.

Before going any further, it is important to emphasize to those who read this book that this literature is to Believers. In this writing, a "Believer" is defined as one who has acknowledged their sin and trust Jesus as Savior. One who by the washing of regeneration and renewing of the Holy Spirit is born again as defined in Scripture (See John 3:3; John 3:16; Titus 3:5 and 1 John 5:10). The "Church" defined is every Believer, the called out ones; the Body of Believers or Body of Christ. In today's culture, word meanings have evolved to mean different things to different people, even in the Church. For example, I met a young lady some time ago and asked her the poignant question, "Are you a Christian?" She replied, "Yes, but I am not saved." The next question I asked was, "Are you *born again?*" She replied, *"No, I didn't say I was born again and all that, I'm just a Christian."* I want the reader to understand the meaning I pour into these words throughout the book.

This book will help Believers recognize popular cultural trends that are contrary to Scripture which have become rather acceptable and common in the Church. The Bible is the most relevant book of all ages! It is never obsolete and its truths endure to all generations. Therefore, it is the trusted source for inspiration from God, and is profitable for doctrine, for reproof, for correction, for instruction in righteousness (2 Timothy 3:16 KJV). This book will canvass common cultural influences in the Church and will shine light from the Scriptures for transformation for those who are "Gripped by the Culture."

Chapter 1

Cultural Christians

Romans 12:2 (AMP)

2 Do not be conformed to this world (this age), [fashioned after and adapted to its external, superficial customs], but be transformed (changed) by the [entire] renewal of your mind [by its new ideals and its new attitude], so that you may prove [for yourselves] what is the good and acceptable and perfect will of God, even the thing which is good and acceptable and perfect [in His sight for you].

Ms. Lu and Mr. Do-Right

Here is a story about a couple I will call them Ms. Lu and Mr. Do-Right. The couple attended a worship service at a church. They appeared to be married as observed by their interactions and behaviors. The Pastor recognized their new faces, so after the benediction, he greeted the couple and engaged in warm conversation. He learned they were not married but were friends. Ms. Lu explained that they had recently met, being introduced to Mr. Do-Right by her best friend. Mr. Do-Right was her best friend's brother recently released from prison. Ms. Lu went on to say that she had been asking God to send her a companion, and she believed that Mr. Do-Right was the answer to prayer. The seasoned and discerning Pastor, understanding the brevity of their knowledge of each other, asked more questions. "What kind of a friend is he and with what kind of benefits does he have as your friend?" Ms. Lu laughed at the humorous question, yet surprised that it was asked seeing they were just meeting. "Are you guys living together and intimately involved?" "Why could he not live with his sister?" They immediately dropped their heads in embarrassment and reiterated their plans to get married. They further explained that Mr. Do-right was not allowed to live with his sister because she did not trust him. They affirmed their need for each other and felt it was okay to live together until ready to make the marriage commitment official. They both said they were Christians. They believed and confessed Jesus as their Savior, so the Pastor asked them to reconcile their behavior in light of the Word of God. They both agreed that it was not in line with the teachings of Scripture, **BUT** felt that God understood. They reasoned there was nothing wrong with what they were doing because they loved each other and were going to get married someday. Mr. Do-Right said that God did not hold them to the "ole fashion" standard of marriage and that they were common-law married as long as he got his mail at Ms. Lu's address. They did not have a problem with what they were doing as Christians. The Pastor explained the error of their way and behavior and encouraged them to make it right before God who loved them. They respectfully listened to the admonition, but casually dismissed the words by saying they were okay and happy in what they believed God was doing.

Unfortunately, this scenario is far too common in the Church but this story is the perfect segue for the definition of a cultural Christian. This story clearly describes Christians who have been discipled by the culture. Some would say these are Christians who have not renewed their minds and simply trapped by the ways of the world. Some would even question if those who think and behave like this are born again? In any case, such noted behavior is dangerous for any person, hence the definition of a cultural Christian.

A Cultural Christian:

1) A cultural Christian is <u>one</u> who is <u>discipled by the culture</u>. One who <u>lives in great deceptions</u>; who filters life through the lens of the world which lets them willfully shape God's revealed Word into whatever they want in order to suit their way of life. They are Christians who live and behave by the dictates of the lower fleshy nature; the world systems of learned behaviors that are common to <u>pop-cultural trends</u> rather than the teachings of the revealed Word of

God. They do not lack knowledge of the Word of God; they simply believe that obeying God's Word is not important because His grace is sufficient even in willful disobedience and rebellion.

Now in light of the definition, let's review the previously mentioned story.

Both Ms. Lu and Mr. Do-Right confesses Jesus as Savior. They are Christians.

- Ms. Lu attended church regularly prayed and asked God for a companion.
- They both had needs: He needed a place to live; she needed companionship. Neither by faith looked to God to meet their needs; they relied on the fleshy nature and their pop-culture worldview.
- They both knew and understood what God expected according to the Word, **BUT** they both felt that God's Word was obsolete as it related to their circumstances.
- They both felt that God understood and would excuse their behavior, besides the culture did not view living together out of wedlock wrong. They simply considered themselves "common-law" married.

Now let's consider these Words of Scripture.

Romans 12:2 AMP

2 *Do not be conformed to this world (this age), [fashioned after and adapted to its external, superficial*

customs], but be transformed (changed) by the [entire] renewal of your mind [by its new ideals and its new attitude], so that you may prove [for yourselves] what is the good and acceptable and perfect will of God, even the thing which is good and acceptable and perfect [in His sight for you].

Ephesians 4:21-24 AMP

21 Assuming that you have really heard Him and been taught by Him, as [all] Truth is in Jesus [embodied and personified in Him],

22 Strip yourselves of your former nature [put off and discard your old unrenewed self] which characterized your previous manner of life and becomes corrupt through lusts and desires that spring from delusion;

23 And be constantly renewed in the spirit of your mind [having a fresh mental and spiritual attitude],

24 And put on the new nature (the regenerate self) created in God's image, [Godlike] in true righteousness and holiness.

Galatians 6:7 AMP

7 Do not be deceived and deluded and misled; God will not allow Himself to be sneered at (scorned, disdained, or mocked by mere pretensions or professions, or by His precepts being set aside.) [He inevitably deludes himself who attempts to delude God.] For whatever a man sows, that and that only is what he will reap.

James 4:17 AMP

17 So any person who knows what is right to do but does not do it, to him it is sin.

God's Goodness and Repentance

Now let's fast forward! After several weeks of the couple meeting with the Pastor, a frantic phone call was received from Ms. Lu. She was in deep sorrow and tears, screaming her request for prayer. She shared Mr. Do-Right had moved on weeks earlier however she had just received a phone call from the Health Department (Prior to <u>HIPAA</u>: Health Insurance Portability and Accountability Act 1996), Mr. Do-Right visited a local health clinic and left Ms. Lu's address and phone information for later contact. He also used her last name (now Mr. Lu). When the health professional called, he stated his urgent need to reach Mr. Lu and disclosed a positive test result for Mr. Do-Right. The health professional disclosed the information believing to be speaking to his wife because the last names were the same. Needless to say Ms. Lu was very shocked by the news and distressed in her new found circumstances. She explained her fears and was advised by the Health Department to be tested. Being overwhelmed and distraught, she could not understand why God would let this happen to her. The Pastor explained that God had nothing to do with her new found circumstance but rather had everything to do with her choices. The Pastor further explained that God loved her and did not want her diseased whether inside or outside of marriage. He reminded her of His love when he admonished them a few weeks earlier. Ms. Lu revisited her behavior with Mr. Do-Right and their cavalier attitude about God's Word. To the Pastor, she acknowledged her wrong behavior, and pop-culture way of thinking and asked for prayer. Through her tears, she asked God's forgiveness for rejecting His truth. Every Believer must understand that God will rescue the rebellious person, but He will never accept a person's rebellion. The Believer, to say it this way, can tie the hand of God when one chooses to participate in rebellion against His Word, even in this dispensation of grace. Rebellion can frustrate grace and hinder its effective work in the life of the Believer. The Pastor prayed and further encouraged her to receive God's forgiveness and believed God for healing and health. Several months later, Ms. Lu contacted the Pastor with a good report on her health. She was rejoicing and back serving the Lord faithfully by her desire and love for the Lord.

It is never a good idea to hold the truth of God's Word and willfully, deliberately and knowingly choose to disobey it. Here are a few of the scripture that helped Ms. Lu get back on course. They will help also if the Holy Spirit is dealing with you in a similar fashion.

Hosea 4:6 AMP

6 My people are destroyed for lack of knowledge; because you [the priestly nation] have rejected knowledge, I will also reject you that you shall be no priest to Me; seeing you have forgotten the law of your God, I will also forget your children.

Romans 2:4 AMP

4 Or are you [so blind as to] trifle with and presume upon and despise and underestimate the wealth of His kindness and forbearance and longsuffering patience? Are you unmindful or actually ignorant [of the fact] that God's kindness is intended to lead you to repent (to change your mind and inner man to accept God's will)?

1 Corinthians 11:31-32 AMP

31 For if we searchingly examined ourselves [detecting our shortcomings and recognizing our own condition], we should not be judged and penalty decreed [by the divine judgment].

32 But when we [fall short and] are judged by the Lord, we are disciplined and chastened, so that we may not [finally] be condemned [to eternal punishment along] with the world.

James 5:15-16 AMP

15 And the prayer [that is] of faith will save him who is sick, and the Lord will restore him; and if he has committed sins, he will be forgiven.

16 Confess to one another therefore your faults (your slips, your false steps, your offenses, your sins) and pray [also] for one another, that you may be healed and restored [to a spiritual tone of mind and heart]. The earnest (heartfelt, continued) prayer of a righteous man makes tremendous power available [dynamic in its working].

1 John 1:9 AMP

9 If we [freely] admit that we have sinned and confess our sins, He is faithful and just (true to His own nature and promises) and will forgive our sins [dismiss our lawlessness] and [continuously] cleanse us from all unrighteousness [everything not in conformity to His will in purpose, thought, and action].

CHAPTER 2

Obedience

"If your theology doesn't change your behavior, it will never change your destiny"... Charles Spurgeon

Romans 6:16 AMP

16 Do you know that if you continually surrender yourselves to anyone to do his will, you are the slaves of him whom you obey, whether that be to sin, which leads to death, or to obedience that leads to righteousness (right doing and right standing with God)?

Now let's talk about obedience. It is a common belief among cultural Christians that obedience to the Word of God is simply something that cannot be achieved. Cultural Christians explain obedience as something that Christ did for us through His death, burial, and resurrection; all anyone has to do is to believe on Jesus Christ, not obey Jesus teachings. Now there is an element of truth, when understood in the proper context of Scripture, as it relates to Salvation which is by grace alone, through faith alone and Christ alone (Eph.2:5-8). Nothing else! The promise of eternal life is given to all who will believe on Jesus, the Christ (John 3:16). However, obedience is the sine qua non that testifies to the grace of God in the born again Believer's life with joy, not dread. Believers are obedient because God's grace supplies ability and desire to obey; not made to obey. No one is made to obey the things of God! True born again Believer's want to, desire to, delight to be pleasing and obedient to things of God. Grace draws the Believer to God's will by faith, which empowers in obedience for service. Consider these scriptures:

Matthew 5:13-14 AMP

13 You are the salt of the earth, but if salt has lost its taste (its strength, its quality), how can its saltiness be restored? It is not good for anything any longer but to be thrown out and trodden underfoot by men.

14 You are the light of the world. A city set on a hill cannot be hidden.

Matthew 5:16 AMP

*16 **Let your light so shine before men** that they may see your moral excellence and your praiseworthy, noble, and good deeds and recognize and honor and praise and glorify your Father Who is in heaven.*

John 14:23-25 AMP

23 Jesus answered, **If a person [really] loves Me, he will keep My word** *[obey My teaching]; and My Father will love him, and* **We will come to him and make Our home** *(abode, special dwelling place) with him.*

24 **Anyone who does not [really] love Me does not observe and obey My teaching.** *And the teaching which you hear and heed is not Mine, but [comes] from the Father Who sent Me.*

25 I have told you these things while I am still with you.

Romans 1:5-6 AMP

5 It is through Him that we have received grace (God's unmerited favor) and [our] apostleship **to promote obedience to the faith and make disciples for His name's sake among all the nations,**

6 And this includes you, called of Jesus Christ and invited [as you are] to belong to Him.

Titus 2:11-12

[11] For the grace of God (His unmerited favor and blessing) has come **forward (appeared) for the deliverance from sin and the eternal salvation for all mankind.**

¹² It has trained us to reject and renounce all ungodliness (irreligion) and worldly (passionate) desires, to live discreet (temperate, self-controlled), upright, devout (spiritually whole) lives in this present world.

Secular and pop-culture make a great effort to mock, ridicule and try to silence Christians who express their heartfelt beliefs and **obedience** to the Word of God. For example, there are well-known Christian Athletes, who have come under fire by unbelievers because they openly express their obedience to their Christian faith. This fire is not just from major news media streams but also Comedians, Late Night Shows, "Family" Sitcoms, and the likes. Have you ever noticed that secular people do not care that you are a Believer or what you believe. They simply **do not want you to demonstrate faith publicly or be obedient** to what your faith teaches, especially if it is true and wholesome. Secular people struggle with athletes who are of the fellowship of the unashamed Believers, because they cannot openly lean too hard to silence them. To do so is to risk cutting off their flow of money because these outstanding Christians Athletes fill their stadiums and arenas and make their fans happy to spend money (1Tim. 6:10). However, secretly they suggest Christian Athletes keep their faith silent and behind closed doors. Thank God for the many Athletes, Entertainers and News Reporters who are openly obedient to their faith in the Lord Jesus Christ and live outwardly by their principles unashamedly!

Mark 8:38

*For whoever is **ashamed** [here and now] **of Me** and My words in this adulterous (unfaithful) and [preeminently] sinful generation, of him will the Son of Man also be **ashamed** when He comes in the glory (splendor and majesty) of His Father with the holy angels.*

This response of the secular and pop-culture is expected, but it is interesting that people who fly the banner of Christianity express their dislike for those who express obedience to their faith in Christ. These are Christians who are gripped by the culture that "entertains" them, rather than the Scriptures that "claims" them. Some people fly the banner of Christianity but have no biblical discipleship, thus meet the definition of the cultural Christian.

Prayer Rally Story!

There was a statewide prayer rally held in Houston, Texas called by the Honorable Rick Perry, who is a Christian, and just so happened to be the Governor of Texas. The State had been experiencing a drought of unprecedented measures. The earth was dry and parched; wildfires were consuming the state in heavily populated areas, and the rivers and lakes were drying up. The farmers and cattlemen were losing economically with great losses of their produce and stocks as well as major cities were on ration notices for water use. Things were beyond the realm of human means. The Honorable Rick Perry met with some of the leading Pastors throughout the State and called a prayer meeting, recognizing that he was a leader with responsibilities yet he understood his frailty as a man. Being a Christian, he believed that the matters of our State were beyond him as a Governor and needed divine intervention. So he, not as the Governor of Texas, but as a humble man and Believer in Jesus Christ asked Pastors and other Spiritual Leaders to join him in praying for our State. The turnout for prayer was one of the biggest in Texas State history.

To the chagrin of some Christians, I learned of their protest after the meeting. They felt that prayer was not appropriate for the Governor to do; unknowingly stating that the U.S. Constitution calls for separation of Church and State. They believed that people ought to pray personally, but not in the public square. Furthermore, they stated that the Governor belonged to everyone and should not have one particular faith of preference, but should be open to all faiths of his constituents. No doubt these Christians were inaccurate in their doctrinal beliefs. The lens through which they view life and make sense of it was the same as the secular arena and pop-culture. Cultural beliefs gripped them.

World Views in a Nutshell

A worldview simply put, is the lens through how one views life and makes sense of it. There are many kinds of worldviews but for the sake of this writing I categorized them below. Christians can be identified in each one of these categories.

Underworld Worldview: People who hold this worldview are **LAWLESS**. There is **NO LAW** that holds them, but the ones they make for themselves. They have no regard for authority or its laws. Their motivations are to get over, manipulate and control. These behaviors are mostly and readily seen in gangs, mafia, white-collar criminals, drug dealers, thieves, thugs and some people who fight and scrape for survival.

Secular Worldview: People who hold this worldview find legal ways to do **immoral** and **unethical** things. Their aim is always lawful, so they often go after the legal systems to change laws to suit their agendas. They use the law to profit with no regard to its effects on others. These are the people who are behind the Abortion Industry, the Homosexual/Gay Agenda, Pornography Industry, and Embryonic Stem Cell Researchers, Organ and Body Parts Harvesting and other watershed moral issues of our culture. They use the law to gain power.

Fundamentals Questions of Morality and Ethic

- Morality ask and answers the question – Would God do it?
- Ethics ask and answers the question – Does this hurt a fellow man?

Many issues that face our nation could be resolved if everyone used this grid of nutshell questions. The Church would be more united in one voice that will infect and affect the culture for righteousness.

Proverbs 14:34 AMP

34 Uprightness and right standing with God (moral and spiritual rectitude in every area and relation) elevate a nation, but sin is a reproach to any people.

Religious Worldview: These are people who see the world through a religious idea. They have a form of godliness but deny the power (2 Tim 3:5). They may attend Church regularly and are often heavily involved with the Church and its functions. Many participate in various auxiliaries such as the Church Choir, Deacon Board, Ushers, Praise/Worship Team and Children's Church Workers. However, they cheat on their taxes and in business. They fornicate, whoremonger, lie, steal, and live ungodly (with justification) on a daily basis with no witness of Christian conviction in their life until Sunday. They teach their children to lie, but not to lie to them. They are often easily recognized by their boisterous talk about the Lord and external wearing of a huge cross, a bumper sticker or some religious symbol. They display a form of godliness but have no real power to live like Christ.

Exhibit A. A deacon smoking a cigarette and drinking a beer one Sunday afternoon. At a church picnic, the deacon said to his son, "Son, I will beat the tar out of you if I ever catch you smoking and drinking!"

Exhibit B. Debt collector calls and the parent instructs the child to answer and say, as they whisper in the background, "Tell them I am not home!" When the call ends, the parent says, "Boy, don't you ever lie to me."

Biblical/Kingdom Worldview: People who hold this worldview strive to live by the living principles of the Bible in every arena of life. This person sees life institutions like family, economic, education, and politics, through lenses of scriptural truths. They believe when acted upon as prescribed in Scripture, one will always gain the best for themselves and the whole of society.

Example: A fellow co-worker commended a supervisor for a major airline regarding her Christian faith. Surprisingly following the commendation came a sarcastic criticism dealing with this biblical worldview. The co-worker said, "I am glad you are a Christian, but you tend to view everything through the Bible when everyone else does not." The co-worker meant it as a subtle insult, but the supervisor saw it as a compliment. A biblical worldview was shining bright! Later, in one of the most difficult times in their life, the co-worker requested prayer and eventually came to know the Lord and apologized saying, "I did not understand, but I understand now." Jesus said these things would happen in the world to those who believed on Him and lived Godly (2 Timothy 3:12).

Now, do not be surprised in knowing that Christians are in all of these worldview categories. It is important for Believers to understand the purpose of salvation through the Lord Jesus Christ. Salvation in Christ Jesus is more than just to escape the penalty of sin that was due us but this salvation should impact and influence a change in the culture. Christians are the salt of the earth and the light of the world. Salt preserves and light illuminates! If what we believe about God does not change our behavior then it will not change our destiny or world. Believers by nature are world changers! The idea behind the gift of preaching is to bring about transformation in minds that shape behaviors for the Kingdom of God. To change a person's behavior, one must change a person's belief system or the lens through how they view life and make sense of it.

I Do Not Want To... Story!

A Christian lady was invited to a social mingle where alcohol was being served. In general conversation, the "social drinking" question about Christians and alcohol came up. The host commented that the Christian lady **"could not"** drink alcohol. Needless to say, the Christian lady used this as a perfect opportunity to share her faith and to lend a little understanding about, "cans and cannot" of Christianity. She simply explained a Christian is free to do anything they want because Christ frees from legalistic duties of "do's" and "don'ts" (1 Corinthians 6:12). She further stated that people often drink for various reasons, none of which she found suitable for her. Thus, she did not drink because she did not **"want to"**. The Christian lady did not drink alcohol as a principle of "will not" rather than "could not". It is a matter of volitional will and choice. Many times Christians blame the devil for things that happen and some even blame God, when the truth of the matter it is neither. We sometimes need to consider our ways. What are we willfully allowing in our lives by commission and participation that does not build up or advance the Kingdom in any way?

Every faithful Believer has the same freedom when they are walking in obedience to the revealed will of God. In the words of the old hymn, "Trust and obey for there's no other way to be happy in Jesus, lest you trust and obey." (Written by John H. Sammie/1887)

Having a Biblical Worldview will guide Believers into a sanctified life and way of living in any environment. Daniel and the three Hebrew boys had this testimony. Taken to a strange land, but their behavior did not change. They were Hebrew boys who worshiped Jehovah even in Babylon. They did not eat the King's meat or drink the King's drink, and they were ten times better. Changing a worldview will revolutionize the culture and change destiny.

Chapter 3

Broken Moral Compass

"Error increases with distance"... Dr. Edwin Louis Cole

Psalm 100:5

5 For the Lord is good; his mercy is everlasting, and his **truth endureth to all generations.** *KJV*

Proverbs 23:23

23 Buy the truth, and sell it not; also wisdom, and instruction, and understanding. KJV

Remembering a story of a Captain, which set sail from an eastern coastal city traveling westward. He carefully planned his trip using various nautical navigational tools like a Gyro Compass, Radar, Speed and Distance Log Devices. He charted his course and was pretty sure to reach his desired destination as charted and on time. He had a partner who traveled with him to help him navigate the journey and they set sail. His partner was to set the remote control navigational tools so to control the ship's steering systems from a remote location, making their journey easier and more carefree. However, the compass was not calibrated to the exact degrees as outlined for the trip. Needless to say, they did not reach their desired destination but was about 400 miles off course. In a review of what went wrong, the Captain discovered that the compass was miscalibrated, and as they progressed in their travel the more off course they became. He noticed that error increased with distance.

Broken Moral Compass

In these times of relativism and political correctness, many people are confused and struggling with truth and have lost their boundaries, unable to recognize the extremes. The pointer on the moral compass is broke in the culture and even after salvation, many want to continue to use that same broken compass in the Church. This idea is not new, but God forbids! After the born again experience, the Apostle Paul encourages all Believers to renew their minds (See Ephesians 4:17-24 AMP). Get rid of the old compass that calls the Church to lighten up on the biblical concepts of God's wrath, sin, repentance, judgment, and hell. Ideas that demand the Church to speak a more positive message of love, acceptance, tolerance, grace and peace to all. Requiring a message of salvation without the Cross, forgiveness without repentance, grace without faith, power without the Holy Ghost, sin remitted without the shedding of blood. The thoughts that everyone is innately good and all should live life to the fullest and do whatever one wants because God understands and is a forgiving God. This compass points to doing anything and everything as long as someone else is not getting hurt. Do it! Do it! Do it until satisfied! Whatever it is, just do it! Then to further convolute the matter, there are some Church leaders who have endorsed such ideas at the altar of "church growth" and "membership" increase. The cliché is, "You have to catch a fish before you can clean it". So let's fill our worship centers up with entertainment to draw the unsaved in and then let's clean them. Sounds good, but the little cliché breaks down when it comes to the spiritual truth. The thought here is to draw the unsaved to church with entertainment bait, and when they bite, we can reel them in. The truth of the matter is that gathering unbelievers to worship God is futile. The Church consist of those who believe, caught, cleaned and "called out!" We are those who are washed in the Blood of the Lamb, who are born again and created in Christ Jesus, by the Word of God. The Church is not the fellowship of the unregenerate who gather together to sing worship songs unto the living God while abiding in spiritual death hoping to fall in love with God. We must rethink this idea. Every believer is to win the lost and then bring them into the fellowship of the called out ones. I realize that unbelievers get in among Believers, but when they do, they do not remain an unbeliever. They will be converted. Please do not dismiss this as legalistic meddling because this cultural trend of "Church" has gripped many. Consider this story.

Just Too Serious Story!

In many Churches today, there are seasons when people come and go, not uncommon for this generation of churchgoers. Most of the time when members move on they do so in the offense, especially when disciplinary matters are administered to bring corrective measures to errors. Because most people perceive church discipline as a punitive act rather than a restorative act, people easily become offended. During times of prayer, the Lord will expose and reveal what is out of order in a local fellowship. It was during this time of prayer and fasting that a Pastor made adjustments that some people did not like. Some even resigned their membership sighting they were not looking for a Pastor who was observing their Christian growth and maturity; because the Pastor encourages biblical discipleship, spiritual growth and obedience to God's Word. One person stated they need a Pastor who did not seriously expect a person to live biblically. They left one church to find another church that was not "so serious" stating, "I do not need to be or want to be encouraged to live a Christian life." Neither did they like nor believe in church discipleship. Church was "too serious." This story ended with this person's life on a junk heap. They were found soliciting men on the internet and had frequent weekend live-ins and eventually ended up heartbroken, feeling empty and devalued by Mr. Sort-of-Kinda.

Although love, acceptance, tolerance, grace, and peace are parts of the Gospel message, we must not omit the Cross, God's wrath, sin, repentance, judgment, and hell. Even though they are not popular messages of today's culture because of unbelief. 2 Corinthians 5:11 says, "Knowing, therefore, the terror of the Lord, we persuade men..." Persuade men to flee from the wrath that is to come upon all those who do not believe. John 3:36 says, "He that believeth on the Son hath everlasting life: and he that believeth not on the Son shall not see life; but **the wrath** of God abideth on him." The incorruptible compass is the Word of God, and it is set and will always point to the righteousness of God. It is always right and will remain the true scale of God's moral standard for the Church and the world now and for generations to come.

Chapter 4

Church and Culture Change

The culture says that times have changed, and the Church must change with the times and need to update God's Word to fit the current culture. However, the Scriptures do not teach this idea of change. Change in the Church has been a big topic in the past 20 years, and the discussion about "old school" versus "new school" church has emerged. Multimedia technologies have changed our world forever thus giving us new methods to distribute the Gospel message. However, the message remains the same. God and His Word did not change! We must not confuse "the message" with "the method."

Matt 24:35 KJV

*35 Heaven and earth shall pass away, but **my words shall not pass away**.*

Malachi 3:6 KJV

6 *For I am the Lord, **I change not**; therefore ye sons of Jacob are not consumed.*

Hebrews 13:8 KJV

*Jesus Christ **the same yesterday, and today, and forever**.*

Church Attendance and the Culture Influence

School Activities Story

When growing up, my parents encouraged us to be involved in extracurricular activities sponsored by the school. There were activities for basketball, football and drill team, and we had full liberty to participate as long as it did not conflict with church activities. The routine was to advise the Coaches that no participation was allowed on Wednesday evenings or Sundays because those were church times. If that was not suitable, we were not allowed to participate. The Coach reply was "no practice" on Wednesday nights and no activities on Sunday because church was a part of their Wednesday's and Sunday's also. Plus, there was no "Activity Bus" that ran after school hours on these days because the bus drivers went to church. Also, the School Board members were in church on Wednesday's and Sunday's. Thus, church attendance were promoted at all levels throughout the culture. MY!!!! Look how things have changed! Church attendance and a wholesome spiritual life were essential to the family and cultural stability. This example shows the Church impact upon the culture where the educational institutions regularly supported participation in worship. It was an essential part throughout the culture.

Fast forward! Pastoring, we have seen church attendance drop to an all time low, during midweek times and one of the main reasons given by parents is youth extracurricular afterschool activities. The cultural influence upon the Church in this area is unprecedented. Church is replaced with hopes of greatness for their children on a professional sports team rather than hope to make it to heaven or have good moral bearings. Too often, we find that parents are trying to re-live their dream or reverse their mistakes through their kids. The facts are in and in reality a very small percentage of all high school athletes make it to college on scholarship, and that number considerably reduces when it comes to the professional teams. In contrast, everyone will make it to eternity. Everyone will face a judgment of eternal life or eternal death. An eternal perspective is the weightier matter of life for the Christian. We must re-examine this in light of biblical truth. What would happen if Christian parents would return to the values of the previous generation and say this child will not participate on Wednesday nights and Sundays because we as a family attend church? What would happen if the Christians did not care about what the culture thinks about their faith? What would happen if Christian parents did not respond to the dictates and whims of their children and parent biblically again; giving direction in things that have eternal gain and value? Consider these Scriptures:

1 Timothy 4:8-9 AMP

8 For physical training is of some value (useful for a little), but godliness (spiritual training) is useful and of value in everything and in every way, for it holds promise for the present life and also for the life that is to come.

9 This saying is reliable and worthy of complete acceptance by everybody.

1 Corinthians 9:25

25 Now every athlete who goes into training conducts himself temperately and restricts himself in all things. They do it to win a wreath that will soon wither, but we [do it to receive a crown of eternal blessedness] that cannot wither. AMP

Chapter 5

Church and the Internet Culture

Cyber- Church Story

One afternoon at a luncheon with some Pastors from the Houston area, the subject of "Cyber Church" came up. The question on the table was, "What is the relevance of the local church in today's world of technology and internet use". To my surprise, some believed that shortly, there will be no need for a local fellowship. Believers will not meet physically because the new meeting place will be in chat rooms online. There will be sermons, prayer, and the ability to give online. Thus, the office of Pastor as we know it will become obsolete; hence the advent of the Cyber-Pastor. The table conversation ended with a real concern of how to remain connected and relevant in the wake of the new world of technology. Cyber Church is not a difficult matter if we view it in light of scripture.

Hebrews 10:25

25 Not forsaking or neglecting to assemble together [as believers], as is the habit of some people, but admonishing (warning, urging, and encouraging) one another, and all the more faithfully as you see the day approaching. AMP

Acts 2:42

42 And they continued stedfastly in the apostles' doctrine and fellowship, and in breaking of bread, and in prayers. (KJV)

Acts 2:42

42 And they steadfastly persevered, devoting themselves constantly to the instruction and fellowship of the apostles, to the breaking of bread [including the Lord's Supper] and prayers. (AMP)

Scriptures answer the question under discussion, giving us a marvelous picture of the behavior of the historical Christian church. Establishing an original intent of the fellowship of Believers coming together (assembly) to encourage steadfast perseverance, devotion to instructions and fellowship. One may argue that you can get all this in a chat room on the internet. However, it lacks the accountability of the seeing eyes of other fellow Believers. The overseeing Pastor and other Ministry Gifts placed in the Body for spiritual growth and maturity to ensure sound doctrine.

Technology Usefulness

Genesis 1:26

And God said, Let us make man in our image, after our likeness: and <u>let them have dominion...</u> over all the earth...

Let us see if we can make sense of our new technical world in light of biblical truth. The Word of God clearly says that mankind is to have dominion over everything on the earth. Dominion means he is to have a sovereign and supreme authority; the power of governing and controlling all things in the earth. Hence, man has the power to direct, control, use and dispose of at pleasure. The right of possession and use of technology is totally in the hands of men. Technology is like money; it is amoral. It is neither good nor evil in and of itself. Man determines whether its use is for good or evil. The exercise of dominion over the earth demands that we build, explore, create, and discover. When a man is doing this, he is most like God revealing and showing forth the true image and likeness of God in which man is created.

Our world today demands technology, and it is here to stay and will advance at a rapid pace. In the past thirty years, our everyday experience with technology has grown so that computers, smart phones, social media, and email are standard parts of our daily lives. It seems like time has sped up, and everything is faster even the days. Life seems to be faster because of such things, and such speed has its downside. These new technologies were supposed to make life simpler and to save time. Ask yourself, how much time is saved? Is there more time to spend with the Lord because of new computer technologies like touch pads, internet, cell phone? There are some days I want to throw my cell phone out of the window to be frank about it. Is there less stress? Are you working more efficiently relieving yourself of overtime work or do you find yourself filling that extra time with something else? It has made me busier. Not to mention other possible physiological impact of technology on the body. For example, an increase of Dry Eye and Restless Leg Syndrome, Carpal Tunnel, Lumbar strains. All believed to be a contributor when long term use and extended hours spent on our helpful, time-saving gadgets. So I'm sure you can see that technology is here to stay, and the Church must embrace it and use it as a tool to propagate the Gospel. After all, technology will play a significant role in end-times before the coming of the Lord and during the tribulation period (Revelation 11:1-13).

In light of this discussion, all technological advances come from God's wisdom and is created for the advancement of the Kingdom of God. Radio, Television, Reel to Reel Tapes, Records, Eight Track Tapes, Cassette Tapes, CDs and now the Internet, are all tools useful to advance Kingdom business. These mediums of communication were never designed to take the place of the local Church but are helpful tools to supplement and enhance the spread of the Gospel message to the masses. Believers ought to take every occasion to dominate and use the most advanced technologies to promote the Kingdom. Again these tools were never intended to take the place of local fellowships, but rather to enhance the local fellowship and the Body of Christ. The idea of Cyber/Tele-Church with Cyber/Tele-Pastors is being entertained by many Believers who are again, gripped by the culture.

Bed-Side Baptist Church Story

Please understand that this next story is no reflection on the Baptist in any way. It is simply noted here to illustrate the previously mentioned idea. You may know, Houston is the fourth (4th) largest City in the country, home to almost 4 million people. Like the vastness of the City, there are vastnesses of churches to choose from in denominations one can hardly count. Just name them, small, medium, large and mega; it can be found in Houston. A church received a phone call requesting a hospital visit for a family member who was not a member of a local fellowship. It is customary for that church to get as much information as possible before making hospital visits especially when the request is from a secondary source. When asked if the requesting person had a local fellowship where they attended regularly, the response was yes!

They said, "Bed-Side Baptist" and "Pastor Pillow" was the Preacher. No doubt the caller was being facetious, but later stated that the patient did not go to a "local church" having attended church on Sunday by television while staying in bed. She named a particular popular TV personality as the patient's Pastor.

No doubt this is unsound thinking. The idea of attending Cyber-Church as a normal practice for a Believer is no doubt the result of improper discipleship. Now, this is not a critique or criticism of any television Minister or Ministry, but simply illustrating the influence of the cultural idea of Cyber/Tele-Church and Cyber/Tele-Pastor amongst Believers and this idea is growing.

The culture says there is no need for the local church since church is available via technology and television. Why waste our time going to a local fellowship with other Believers when there is the convenience of church at home, and can claim a television and internet personality for Pastor? After all, "God does not care." What a strange way of thinking! When one is healthy and able bodied, the Cyber/Tele-Church/Pastor is the convenient choice. However, when one became "sick and shut-in" and unable to get out, a local church and Pastor becomes the convenient choice. The need to be touched by a "real person" becomes very important. It seems that in circumstances like times of "shut-in", it is most appropriate and a good time for a Cyber/Tele-Church or Cyber/Tele-Pastor. Situations like these merit some spiritual edification to come via multimedia streams reaching into hospital rooms, nursing homes, etc. encouraging and building up the Body. These are ideal times for the Cyber/Tele-Church. However, the Believer that connects with a local fellowship have the best of both worlds. A caring local church family and the encouraging and fortifying works of the Cyber/Tele-Church. Attending a local church with other Believers should be the norm of Christian worship. Again, when using a miscalibrated compass, the error increases with distance. Let's bring the compass back in balance. Encourage every Believer to have a local fellowship and attend there regularly for spiritual growth and enrichment while understanding that Cyber/Tele -Ministers are not to take the place of the local church.

Chapter 6

Church and the Culture "Dress Codes"

1 Corinthians 10:31 (KJV)

[31] Whether therefore ye eat, or drink, or **whatsoever ye do, do all to the glory of God**.

Preparing for Sunday Worship

Growing up, Sunday Worship began on Saturday afternoons and, for the most part, every child in our community had the same routine. Saturday mornings was time for chores, a must before we could play with our friends. Laundry, bedrooms and bathrooms cleaned, yard work, and haircuts (boys) completed before playtime of touch football, kickball, basketball and recreational gym. We were free to play throughout the community until dusk; at that time we had to return home to prepare for Sunday Worship. This routine looked like this. Ironing clothes, polishing shoes, (girls) hair washed and neatly set for curls, and clothing were all laid out in homework for Sunday. The idea of all this preparation was to give God our best. We had Sunday clothes, Sunday shoes and a Sunday attitude on Saturday evening. When Sunday morning came, the gospel music would play, and everything was done decently and in order. Mother would not allow Sunday morning chaos. We were ready to go into the house of the Lord in Sunday best, and everything done in devotion unto the Lord. We were required to go to church neatly groomed and in our absolute Sunday best. It was considered our reasonable service and worship unto the Lord.

Today's church culture is so entrenched with the world that skimpy and scantily clad attire is acceptable as "the style" that is a reflection of the all-time low in basic grooming in America's culture. Lowering the standard of dress codes has ever so subtly crept into the church under the disguise of "come as you are." It seems like the Church struggles to get this right. The pendulum swings from one extreme to the other. It goes from no make-up, no jewelry, no pants, to letting it all hangout. Risqué fashions reflect mostly on women because of the Fashion Industry as a whole. It is marketing that drives women fashion and designers who create clothing styles around the fundamentals of attraction, sensuality and money (what sells?). In the culture, sex sells even in the clothing industry.

Unfortunately, many of the top fashion designers in the world practice various lifestyles and have great influence in the clothing industry. So with "sexy" selling, designers make clothing for where the money is being made. Many facets of the clothing industry are equally responsible and guilty of selling sex and pornography in the culture. These marketing trends have trickled down to the teenage girls and even elementary girls, so it starts early. Women are marketed to believe that risqué is the look of beauty in pop fashion. Unfortunately many Christian women have bought into the "sexy diva" idea, a concept forged in the bowels of worldly sensuality and youthful lust. What an atrocity for women (Believers or non-Believers) to be merchandised in this way and sacrificed on the altar of "sexy," a cheap substitute for real beauty. What's the solution? The answer is the Word of God and basic common sense. Let's start with God's Word first then we will look at those things that make common sense.

1 Corinthians 14:40 (KJV)

⁴⁰ *Let all things be done **decently and in order**.*

1 Timothy 2:9 (KJV)

⁹*In like manner also, **that women adorn themselves in modest apparel**, with shamefacedness and sobriety; not with broided hair, or gold, or pearls, or costly array;*

Titus 2:3-4 (KJV)

*3 The aged women likewise, that they **be in behaviour as becometh holiness**, not false accusers, not given to much wine, teachers of good things;*

*4 That they may **teach the young women to be sober**, to love their husbands, to love their children,*

1 Peter 3:5 (AMP)

*5 For it was thus that **the pious women of old who hoped in God were [accustomed] to beautify themselves** and were submissive to their husbands [adapting themselves to them as themselves secondary and dependent upon them].*

Common Sense Screen

The beauty of all creation lets us know that God is a designer of beauty! Christian men and women should embrace the idea of modesty rather than the world's idea of sexy. Make-up and basic skin care is acceptable to help nourish the skin and keep it looking radiant and beautiful as well. Remember Esther had a beauty treatment for one year. Ladies ought to pamper and retrain the mind in God's beauty aids from the Word of God. Let's crucify the ideas of the world about "sexy" and embrace God's vision of beauty. It is important to understand the agenda of worldliness and choose not to participate in it and look for styles that are fitting instead of sensual. There are professional who can assist in suitable wardrobe, hair, accessorizing, and makeup selections. Also, remember that a good respectable friend can give some tips in this area also. Above all let's get back to the basic art of personal grooming and simply strive to look the best! Moreover, by all means, before stepping out, LOOK IN THE MIRROR! Evaluate yourself for public decency; watch the hemlines and the necklines. Listen to the Holy Spirit, who is the great Teacher. He will teach in all things.

Now, some reading this may think these are prudish, ole fashion, legalistic and bondage ideas that have nothing to do with New Testament redemptive truths. That is fair to think, however, this is written for self-evaluation and to inspire change in practical things that is affecting the Church.

Let's examine this fact for understanding. Fashion is about the appeal and speaks for and about people in industry of all sorts. Clothing appeals to others, especially those of the opposite sex and gives identity. Fashion designers work hard to produce fashion with sex appeal because this is what sells. Most ladies lack understanding in the fact that men wrestle with thousand of sexual images every day. Images seen in every form of media (TV, Internet, Billboards, Magazines, Newspapers, Commercial, Man Caves Talks, Sitcoms, etc.) and seen on skimpily dressed women in the culture adding even more to their struggle. Women, unknowingly and unintentionally, contribute to the pornography industry. This industry has gripped many men in the church who struggle and suffer in silence while dealing with the guilt, the shame and the hiding as the result of insatiable appetites of sexual lust. This is what woman must understand, men are creatures of sight and logic and have a "total recall" button. They are easily sexually motivated by what they see and can recall images in their minds like a gallery app on a cell phone. "Total Recall" was placed in man when God created him. Like God, a man has a natural bent to appreciate things that are beautiful especially a woman. Man's natural bent is not an evil thing because God called His creation of man good and placed this desire in him for a woman, more specifically his wife. God's idea was that a man would desire his woman (wife) and have "Total Recall" for her and her alone. However, something happened called sin. Now with the sin factor introduced into the human experience, man desire for his woman (wife) is not enough. He must now deliberately work to keep in bounds the innate urges for other women. *Job 31:1 says, "I made a covenant with mine eyes; why then should I think upon a maid?"* Consider this scripture in Job who made a covenant with his eyes and mind so as to not look or think upon a woman with lust. Making a covenant is what Christian men must do with their eyes and mind to not look upon a woman. However, this is not so easy to do when sensual images are so pervasive in the culture and even in the Church.

Some men express their struggle with lust and how hard it is to guard their eyes and keep them pure during the week. Some have said that when it comes to the Church, they expect ladies to dress differently. They admit their struggles with pornography and unnatural lust and desire to be free, but find it hard because of the sensual images they see daily in the culture and now when they come to church. They get completely distracted and find it difficult to draw their thoughts into worship. A real eye opener! Herein is modesty, the love of God! Women can make a simple adjustment to help Christian brothers who wrestle in this area. We should strive to make our places of Worship a safe place for men to worship freely without being tripped by stumbling blocks.

Romans 14:13

13Let us not therefore judge one another any more: **but judge this rather, that no man put a stumbling block or an occasion to fall in his brother's way.**

Being fashionable and modestly dressed without the edge of the world's idea of sexy, is critical and most important for Christian women. We are not to be conformed to the world ideas and philosophies. A great blessing comes with biblical thinking and behaving. It frees us from being gripped by the culture.

Chapter 7

Church and the Sensual Culture

"The preacher should not mention such a subject as fornication." My answer to that remark is, "Then you should not commit such iniquity, and give me reason to speak of it."

Charles Spurgeon

Sensuality in the Church

This subject is one of the most relevant to be addressed by the Church seeing that sensuality is at an all-time high throughout the culture touching every facet of our society. America as a nation has become crazed with sensuality and sex stemming from the last wave of the 1950's and 1960's "sexual revolution." This period in American history typifies a dramatic shift in sexual behaviors. Many young people left traditional biblical values inside the protected boundaries of marriage and embraced a more socially acceptable idea of sexual behaviors. It was a time when the political and social norms were challenged unfortunately by a vocal group of minorities. The pulpits in America went silent and thus the Church became irrelevant in the culture during a crucial time in our Nation's history. Sounds familiar? The Vietnam War and the Civil Rights Movement brought even more mixed emotions that fostered distrust for leadership. Beloved leaders were assassinated like President John F. Kennedy (1963), Senator Robert Kennedy (1968) and Martin Luther King Jr. (1968). America's colleges and universities filled with young people trying to find their place in the world with leaders they no longer trusted. So they trusted themselves. Does this sound familiar? The Women's Liberation movement was also on the playing field scoring points for women's freedom. Their cry was to free women from tyrannical ideas like men being the head of women and womanhood equal to manhood thus women needed no head or boss. Among other things, this movement minimized men and their roles in the culture while giving women rights to sexual freedom of expression like men without being labeled. So, some women burned their Bibles, burned their bosses and burned their bra, opening up a national debate about traditional family values. The unfortunate thing was that few Christian women added their salt to the public debate. Thus God was left out again, the Church giving no voice in the culture. Neither did Christian men engage in the debate and the Church was silenced. The anti-biblical secular worldview took center stage in the culture. Sounds familiar? Couple these movements with the spreading drug culture of marijuana, heroin, and cocaine that had become more mainstream, together became the potent cocktail for a "revolution". The Politicians who currently hold offices today are the youth of yesterday's 1950's and 1960's potent revolutions in America, and they continue to stray further from the truth, God, and His Word. Hence, we understand the challenges we face in our culture today. Vladimir Lenin, the founder of the Russian Communist Party, leader of the Bolshevik Revolution, said, "Give me just one generation of youth, and I'll transform the whole world." Although the philosophy of Lenin's communistic views were far-fetched, this statement speaks volume for truth. Read Judges 2:10, and see that happened to Israel in one generation. A nation needs but one generation to get off course, and an entire nation can be swept into total error and chaos. Today in America we see the impact of the 1950's and 1960's "sexual revolution". We now have sexual immorality in ways unimaginable. Human trafficking, sex slavery, and pornography is a multi-billion dollar industry. Playboy Clubs and Swing Houses, Victoria Secrets, and Lingerie Fashion Shows on prime time television, homosexuality making mainstream demands, even to the desire to change the traditional definition of marriage. With all of this going on in the culture, the Church remains to be the only institution that have the answer and deliverance for those who are sexually broken. The Gospel of Jesus Christ is the power of God unto Salvation to all who will believe. We must declare what the Word of God says to refute the darkness and redeem the time for generations to come. The Church cannot afford to sit this one out! The pulpits must re-ignite and address this sensual and sexually engaged culture that have crept into the Church also. In some mainline denominations, homosexuality is acceptable even in the leadership. So let's look at the answers from the Word of God. Consider these Scriptures:

Matthew 15:19

*19For out of the heart proceed evil thoughts, murders, adulteries, **fornications**, thefts, false witness, blasphemies:*

Mark 7:21

*21For from within, out of the heart of men, proceed evil thoughts, adulteries, **fornications**, murders...*

1 Corinthians 6:13

*13Meats for the belly, and the belly for meats: but God shall destroy both it and them. Now the **body is not for fornication,** but for the Lord, and the Lord for the body.*

Corinthians 6:18

[18]*Flee fornication. Every sin that a man doeth is without the body; but he that committeth fornication sinneth against his own body.*

1 Corinthians 7:2

[2]*Nevertheless, **to avoid fornication**, let every man have his own wife, and let every woman have her own husband.*

1 Corinthians 10:8

[8]*Neither let us **commit fornication**, as some of them committed and fell in one day three and twenty thousand.*

Galatians 5:19

[19]*Now the works of the flesh are manifest, which are these; **Adultery, fornication**, uncleanness, lasciviousness,*

Ephesians 5:3

[3]*But **fornication, and all uncleanness**, or covetousness, let it not be once named among you, as becometh saints;*

Colossians 3:5

*⁵Mortify therefore your members that are upon the earth; **fornication, uncleanness, inordinate affection**, evil concupiscence, and covetousness, which is idolatry:*

1 Thessalonians 4:3

*³For this is the will of God, even your sanctification, that **ye should abstain from fornication**:*

Jude 1:7

*⁷Even as Sodom and Gomorrha, and the cities about them in like manner, **giving themselves over to fornication**, and going after strange flesh, **are set forth for an example, suffering the vengeance of eternal fire**.*

Unger's Bible Dictionary says:

FORNICATION (Gk. porneia). Use of illicit sexual intercourse in general (Acts 15:20, 29; 21:25; cf. 1 Cor. 5:1; 6:13, 18; 7:2; etc.). It is distinguished from "adultery" (Gk. moicheia, in Matt. 15:19; Mark 7:21). The NIV usually translates porneia as "sexual immorality" and moicheia as "adultery." Adultery is the term used for such an act when the person is married and fornication when unmarried, and fornication may also be defined as lewdness of an unmarried person of either sex.

Solomon was right to say that there is nothing new under the sun. Jesus and Paul addressed the issue of fornication. To the Church, Paul wrote that the will of God is that Believers abstain from fornication. Fornication is the arching word that includes all immoral sexual behaviors. However, so as not to offend, in today's church culture, the word "fornication" is not an acceptable term to used within the Church. Growing number across a broad spectrum of denominations have chosen not to use the word at all, but rather make things more palatable for the hearer. So they use words like "the sexually challenged" or "sexually broken." Again this is another grip on the Church that has subtly crept in. Make it palatable. The familiarity with sin will not be so comfortable for the Believer if we call sin what the Bible calls it. Especially for those who see sexual immorality as a casual vice of the flesh that God overlooks. Understand that if this gospel is an offense, it is an offense to those who believe not. Let us not think it a strange thing that people are offended at the preaching of the Gospel. There were many who were offended at Jesus' preaching and turned away, and many were offended at the preaching of Paul's message of repentance and Grace. Everywhere Paul went, there was no small stir. In today's culture and even within the Church many do not like this kind of teaching and preaching. There is be no small stir when it happens because the culture has gripped the Church.

Church and the "Hook-Up" Culture

2 Timothy 3 (KJV)

¹This know also, that in the last days perilous times shall come.

²For men shall be lovers of their own selves, covetous, boasters, proud, blasphemers, disobedient to parents, unthankful, unholy,

³Without natural affection, trucebreakers, false accusers, incontinent, fierce, despisers of those that are good,

⁴Traitors, heady, high-minded, lovers of pleasures more than lovers of God;

⁵Having a form of godliness, but denying the power thereof: from such turn away.

In this culture of the "Millennial" generation's, freestyle has become the order of the day. Millennials have typically been characterized by having a strong sense of community (locally and globally), confidence, tolerance, entitlement, self-absorbed, self-obsessed, conceited and egotistical. Not all millennials will fit this predictable grid, but most do. They are known as "Generation Me" and at best estimates, there is approximately 80 million of them, out populating the "Baby Boomers" generation. They are more likely to embrace deceptions because they are driven emotionally and are moved by how they feel rather than what makes rational and logical sense. Hence out of this backdrop comes the birth of the "hook-up" culture.

What is the "Hook-Up"?

The "Hook-up" is any casual sexually intimate activity. It can be as benign as an innocent kiss, or as in-depth as intercourse. What defines it is that it is impromptu, unplanned, impulsive, with no commitment, sometimes with no knowledge of the engaging individuals. It often involves alcohol or drugs and little to no talking. At the conclusion, no one is responsible. This behavior is most popular with college-age young adults, and it is trickling down to the high school level and yes, even to middle school levels.

The brokenness that comes from the poor choices of those who participate in this behavior is unprecedented. Often time participates have testified of their disdain of the practice and hate themselves afterward for participating in it. Men and women alike have expressed the same feelings of shame, guilt, fear, confusions, and lack of love for themselves the other person whom they may never know or ever see again. Participation happens because it feels right at the moment. This vain, superficial way of living is clearly a set up by Satan to kill, steal and destroy, and this behavior is operating in the Church. Hence, we are seeing the rise of more family destruction among

Believers. The impact of this behavior in the Church has a profound effect on the culture. The World has no place to turn to if the Church is equal in immorality as the world who spun such vices. What's the solution? Believers must return to their first love! Remember from where thou have fallen, and repent, and do the first works.

Matthew 15:19

For out of the heart proceed evil thoughts, murders, adulteries, fornications, thefts, false witness, blasphemies:

Mark 7:21

For from within, out of the heart of men, proceed evil thoughts, adulteries, fornications, murders...

1 Corinthians 6:13

Meats for the belly, and the belly for meats: but God shall destroy both it and them. Now the body is not for fornication, but for the Lord, and the Lord for the body.

Corinthians 6:18

[18]Flee fornication. Every sin that a man doeth is without the body; but he that committeth fornication sinneth against his own body.

1 Corinthians 7:2

²Nevertheless, to avoid fornication, let every man have his own wife, and let every woman have her own husband.

1 Corinthians 10:8

⁸Neither let us commit fornication, as some of them committed and fell in one day three and twenty thousand.

Galatians 5:19

¹⁹Now the works of the flesh are manifest, which are these; Adultery, fornication, uncleanness, lasciviousness,

Ephesians 5:3

³But fornication, and all uncleanness, or covetousness, let it not be once named among you, as becometh saints;

Colossians 3:5

⁵Mortify therefore your members which are upon the earth; fornication, uncleanness, inordinate affection, evil concupiscence, and covetousness, which is idolatry:

1 Thessalonians 4:3

³For this is the will of God, even your sanctification, that ye should abstain from fornication:

"Every darkness has its own power. You have to come against that power. Homosexualism is a demon spirit and you have to come against that spirit."

Rev. Lester Sumrall

Homosexuality in the Church

One of the watershed issues of the day is homosexuality in the Church. Unfortunately, small wars have erupted in the Church with much confusion around this issue. Satan is the power behind it all. Many have become more accepting of this practice for various reasons. Like sympathy for a family members who have embraced the lifestyle; for fear of being labeled homophobe, hater, bigot, judgmental, critical or in an operation like musicians, choir member, or administrator. There is a myriad of reasons as to why this has become acceptable by the Church, and one sure reason is that the culture has gripped the Church. God's Word is clear on this subject. Thus, we have a solution. So let's look at it!

Homosexuality is sexual desire or behavior directed toward a person or persons of one's sex. It is prohibited by God and is an abomination according to Leviticus 18:22. People who participate in these behaviors are called homosexuals and develop a strong, unnatural lust for sodomical acts although all may not actively participate in such acts. It is sin and confusion in the way of the soul of a person. It is one of the most difficult behaviors to deal with because of the mind, the will and the emotional ties to its learned behaviors. As a matter of fact, this is true with any immoral sexual behaviors (I Corinthians 6:18). Sexual confusion can begin at a very young age and develop over a period. Whatever the reason is as to why this happens to people, the Scriptures reveals homosexual acts as unnatural and against God's order of nature. Some believe that such behavior stem from unseen evil influences that do not originate with mankind. The message of the Church is that Jesus Christ sets men free. Laboring with those who desire to be free most often takes time and deliverance is not always instantaneous.

The Church Argument

The argument in the Church is whether or not a born again Believer can be in bondage to this or any oppressive spirits. Why argue with doctrine when a person needs freedom from the powers of darkness? Don't argue doctrine, set the person free! Jesus said in Luke 4:18 (KJV), "*The Spirit of the Lord is upon me, because he hath anointed me to preach the gospel to the poor; he hath sent me to heal the brokenhearted, to preach deliverance to the captives, and recovering of sight to the blind, to set at liberty them that are bruised.*" Then the argument swings to the questions of "is it sin?" or "sickness?" to "don't judge." The Bible answers these questions. The Bible states clearly in five places that homosexual behavior is a sin, unacceptable before a Holy God, and God's judgment is upon it. Keep in mind that the biblical definition of sin is missing the mark or standard. The standard is God's Holiness. Reference other translations for more clarity on the following scriptures.

Leviticus 18:22 (KJV)

22 Thou shalt not lie with mankind, as with womankind: it is abomination.

Leviticus 18:22 (GNT)

22 No man is to have sexual relations with another man; God hates that.

Leviticus 20:13 (KJV)

13 If a man also lie with mankind, as he lieth with a woman, both of them have committed an abomination: they shall surely be put to death; their blood shall be upon them.

Leviticus 20:13 (GNT)

13 If a man has sexual relations with another man, they have done a disgusting thing, and both shall be put to death. They are responsible for their own death.

Romans 1:26-27 (KJV)

[26]For this cause God gave them up unto vile affections: for even their women did change the natural use into that which is against nature:

[27]And likewise also the men, leaving the natural use of the woman, burned in their lust one toward another; men with men working that which is unseemly, and receiving in themselves that recompense of their error which was meet.

Romans 1:26-27 (GNT)

[26]Because they do this, God has given them over to shameful passions. Even the women pervert the natural use of their sex by unnatural acts. [27] In the same way the men give up natural sexual relations with women and burn with passion for each other. Men do shameful things with each other, and as a result they bring upon themselves the punishment they deserve for their wrongdoing.

Romans 1:26-27 Amplified Bible (AMP)

[26]For this reason God gave them over and abandoned them to vile affections and degrading passions. For their women exchanged their natural function for an unnatural and abnormal one,

[27]And the men also turned from natural relations with women and were set ablaze (burning out, consumed) with lust for one another—men committing shameful

acts with men and suffering in their own [a]bodies and personalities the inevitable consequences and penalty of their wrong-doing and going astray, which was [their] fitting retribution.

1 Corinthians 6:9-10 (KJV)

[9]*Know ye not that the unrighteous shall not inherit the kingdom of God? Be not deceived: neither fornicators, nor idolaters, nor adulterers, nor effeminate, nor abusers of themselves with mankind,*

[10]*Nor thieves, nor covetous, nor drunkards, nor revilers, nor extortioners, shall inherit the kingdom of God.*

1 Corinthians 6:9-10(AMP)

[9]*Do you not know that the unrighteous and the wrongdoers will not inherit or have any share in the kingdom of God? Do not be deceived (misled): neither the impure and immoral, nor idolaters, nor adulterers, nor those who participate in homosexuality,*

[10]*Nor cheats (swindlers and thieves), nor greedy graspers, nor drunkards, nor foulmouthed revilers and slanderers, nor extortioners and robbers will inherit or have any share in the kingdom of God.*

1 Timothy 1:9-10 (KJV)

[9]*Knowing this, that the law is not made for a righteous man, but for the lawless and disobedient, for the ungodly and for sinners, for unholy and profane, for*

murderers of fathers and murderers of mothers, for manslayers,

[10]For whoremongers, for them that defile themselves with mankind, for menstealers, for liars, for perjured persons, and if there be any other thing that is contrary to sound doctrine;

(Note: 1Timothy 1:10, Sexual lust and fantasy, both homosexual and heterosexual, are sinful according to God's Word.)

1 Timothy 1:9-10 (NET Bible)

[9]realizing that law is not intended for a righteous person, but for lawless and rebellious people, for the ungodly and sinners, for the unholy and profane, for those who kill their fathers or mothers, for murderers,[10] sexually immoral people, practicing homosexuals, kidnappers, liars, perjurers—in fact, for any who live contrary to sound teaching.

The Bible's first revealing on this subject appears in Genesis 18:16-32, 19:1-27 at Sodom and Gomorrah. We see some truths about this sin in that the outcry of it is great, and the sin is grievous unto the Lord. God had it investigated by two messengers. This sin had permeated the entire twin cities; it had become intrinsic within the culture. Homosexuality was accepted by most of the entire city's population so much so that a great number came to have unnatural sexual relations with Lot's guest. Lot offered his virgin daughters in exchange for the protection of his guest. However, this offer was rejected. The men desired sexual relations with other men. God destroyed the Cities after this encounter that proved out the investigation to be true as was also witness by the outcry unto God. Some Christian have a problem with these passages of Scripture because of their human sentiment in thinking that God was brutal to destroy so many, and they hear the cry of today's culture for compassion and tolerance. They become ensnared by their thinking and become sympathizers for the wrong, leaving God out and Satan comes in to further deceive. Hence, Christians find themselves disagreeing with God and giving place to the devil in their words, deeds and actions. The Church must not confuse compassion for those ensnared in homosexuality with acceptance and agreement with their behavior. The Church has no need to be afraid of this subject because there is a biblical answer, and it is through our Lord Jesus Christ. He can and will set the sexually broken free.

The Remedy

First and foremost trust the leading of the Holy Spirit in prayer about the matter. Seek the Lord until clear directions is given because every case is different. The Holy Spirit will guide through any course of deliverance. Second, we must call homosexuality what it is, sin and agree with God and His Word on the subject. Third, Understand that deliverance may not be instantaneous, but most often time includes a process for the total man, the Spirit, the Soul (reason, will and emotion) and the Body. Remember one cannot disciple a demon or cast out the flesh. So those bound must be set free and delivered from the spiritual oppression of homosexuality that drives the lust and confusion (Matthew 8:16; Mark 16:17). Afterward, they must be born again according to the Word of God and by the Holy Spirit (John 3:7). Followed by biblical discipleship in righteousness for a renewed mind (Romans 12:1-2), and the Body presented unto God (1 Corinthians 6:20). The real struggle of deliverance takes place in the renewing of the mind and the presentation of the body. Laboring with a person in this season takes much prayer and accountability. The mind and flesh will often cry for the familiar and crave to be satisfied. All cravings must be resisted to break its power over the mind and flesh. With the fast pace world we live in, the Church has mislaid its desire to work with people until they become completely free and able to stand and resist the fiery darts of Satan.

If a Believer is struggling in this area of sexual brokenness, whether it is homosexuality, sexual promiscuities, pornography, pedophilia, Jesus can and will set free! Do not suffer in silence any longer. Get free of deceit and in full disclosure denounce it before a Holy God who sees and knows. There is no time to be ashamed; know that this is the tool of Satan to keep his captive grip. Connect with and be accountable to a mature Bible believing Pastor and church, who can minister in this area and rally to set free anyone who desires to be free from this bondage.

Family! What to do practically?

Many people are troubled when a family member, Pastor, Church Leaders, Politician, and Coaches break their silence and announce their involvement and embrace of the homosexual lifestyle. The Church often does not know what to do practically. No doubt this can be disheartening to any Bible believing person or family. Such announcement can be devastating bringing out a wellspring of malevolent emotions that range from anger to resentment, rejection and disownment, silence and abandonment, confusion and mistreatment. Coupled with the flood of emotions comes the bombardment of questions like, why this family? How did this happen? When did this start? What did we do wrong? Where did we miss it? Who is the blame? Followed then by tears and prayers and somehow through the pain of it all come to the conclusion that it is a family member that you love dearly. Then you wonder how to respond, seeing they have rejected the natural order of sexual expression and taken up homosexuality. How do one interact with family members in their new way of life? How to balance this love and hate relationship? Love the person but hate what they do. How to practically remain in a relationship with a family member without compromising faithfulness to God?

What does one do in seasons of believing God for their deliverance and living by faith; while casting not away confidence as one wait for the great recompense of reward (Hebrew 10:35-37)? What to do when love one says, "Acceptance of me is to accept my lifestyle." "To love me is to embrace the real me and who I am in my confusion." "You cannot say that you love me and not love what I am all about." "You cannot love me and not embrace and love the people whom I love." What to do? What to say? These are all tough questions and easily resolved and requires honest and straight dialog. These feeling are also real in such cases of infidelity in marriage. Same emotion and questions arise.

First understand that homosexuality did not originate with your love one. It is a snare of the devil by which people become entangled. One wants to blame someone, blame the devil not yourself or the ensnared person. Remember we wrestle not against flesh and blood but powers of darkness (Ephesians 6:12). These powers of darkness seek to manifest themselves through humanity and the more a person participates in darkness, the greater the stronghold and the greater the expression. The just lives by faith (Hebrews 10:38) and you cannot be moved by what you see. Satan is defeated in the arena of faith. Make it a point to pray fervently and continually based on the Word of God. Listen to the Holy Spirit's guidance in everything. Be consistent! Don't worry about what people will think. Don't be ashamed of another person's choice. It is their choice, not your choice you made for them.

Second, realize that many find themselves ensnared and confused by the powers of darkness. Since they are ensnared, do not become like them by participating and sanctioning their rebellion and wrong choices. Verbally, without deception, express love. Communicate openly and lovingly your disappointment in their choice while at the same time respect their right to choose. Every human being is a free moral agent created in God's image and likeness and will give an account for themselves. Sincerely convey, as a Believer in the Word of God, you will never be able to embrace or condone their lifestyle choice. Not accepting their lifestyle is often seen as a lack of love so be sure to explain your position is centered in faith that you can not and will not abandon because of their choice. Clearly articulate your resolve is not to be confused with lack of love for them. Simply you are letting them know your position on the issue and ask them to respect your right to choose Biblical truth to live by even as you respect their right to choose. Also, stress a willingness to pray for them to be free from their bondage.

Third, set rules for respect for home and family relationships. Don't be afraid to ask for respect in your home and relationship with them. Articulate what that respect should resemble. For example, you might welcome the family member home at all times however their partners are not welcome. This same thing would be requested in cases of marital infidelity. A loved one may find this offensive and may choose not to come to the home in protest to punish. They may decide punishment by silence and not to speak again. The spiritual warfare may begin to manifest more. Understand the fight and the wrestling not with flesh and blood, but against spiritual darkness. Strive to keep open communication, even through times of unseemly actions. Choose to call them or drop them a love note. Continue to stand your ground and reaffirm your love for them. Reiterate they are always welcome home but the rules remain the same. You may make a similar policy by asking them to respect family time. Live by the set or structured policies to maintain peace. For those who have family that resides in the home, rules should remain as usually. You will need to add or alter policy and again, ask them not to breach trust by breaking the established rules. Have consequences for the rule breakers. Discuss how crucial this matter is and let expectations be known and made clear.

Fourth, do not battle alone. Inform a Pastor, Prayer Partner or Prayer Team about the fight for your love ones deliverance from sexual immorility. Have them unite in prayers and fasting. Find scripture that covers what you are believing God for and declare it in Jesus name, keeping in mind that there is no distance in the spirit. Satan hears the word of God and tremble. Tell Satan he cannot have your love one and call that love one by name. Declare their freedom from Satan's power and call them out of that lifestyle. Tell Satan he can no longer hold them captive to his deception and power. Break his power and assignment over the life of your loved one. Do not stop! Keep releasing faith by speaking faith-filled words and standing on the promises of God for your love one.

Fifth, develop a life of Praise. Praise God for the victory before you see it. This releases the power of God. Praise God radically for His faithfulness to His Word for He hasten to perform His Word when we believe Him. Don't wait until the battle is over, shout now! For your know in the end, YOU WIN! Praise will keep you in the arena of faith. It will keep your mind lifted and quenches the darts of Satan. Keep praising God for His promises concerning the seed of the righteous.

Chapter 8

It's My Body, I Can Do What I Want!

1 Corinthians 6:20 (KJV)

²⁰For ye are bought with a price: therefore glorify God in your body, and in your spirit, which are God's.

In recent times, many arguments have been raised by the issue of a person's right to choose. What one can or cannot do with their body while some argue that State and Government have a right to. However, there are those who say State has no right to intrude in such matters because the State or Government do not give such rights. The language of the Kingdom or members of the Body of Christ are different on all points because Believers submit to a Biblical worldview. We understand that God our Father is the creator and He alone has every right to give instruction as to what we should and should do in our bodies and life. In scripture, Believers are encouraged to glorify God in their bodies (1 Corinthians 6:20). 1 Thessalonians 5:23 (KJV), says, "And the very God of peace sanctify you wholly; and

I pray God your whole spirit and soul and body be preserved blameless unto the coming of our Lord Jesus Christ." This passage of Scripture reveals a man in his total creation as a three-part being. He is a spirit, he has a soul, and he lives in a body and the Apostle Paul says the God of peace sanctify man completely. Every part of man is sanctified, spirit, soul and body. To sanctify mean to set apart, to be declared holy, consecrated. Every Believer should know that God has set apart and declared sacred the total man that includes the body. In knowing this, we then conclude that we are not at liberty to just do anything that we feel like in our bodies or to our bodies. Our bodies are a sacred tool in which the human spirit and the Holy Spirit resides (1 Corinthians 6:19-20). We are to present our bodies a living sacrifice holy and acceptable unto God this is our reasonable service (Romans 12:1). The whole man belongs to God!

Tattooing (Tats), Body Piercing, and Gauging

Leviticus 19:28(KJV)

28Ye shall not make any cuttings in your flesh for the dead, nor print any marks upon you: I am the Lord.

Tattooing and body piercing has been practiced among human cultures since the ancient times. Ancient Middle Eastern, Egyptian and African cultures have participated in tattooing, cuttings and body piercing for various reasons like cultural beliefs and customs, superstitious ideas and religious reasons associated with pagan worship. We see an example of this practiced when Elijah addresses the prophets of Baal on Mt Carmel (1 Kings 18:1-40). They cut themselves calling upon their God (1 Kings 18:28).

Here in Leviticus 19:28-30, we see God's prohibition and instruction to the Children of Israel regarding the practice of cutting and marking the body which were customs practiced by other nations who worshipped idols. The Law of God prohibited all pagan religious customs including pagan mourning rites that required piercing or cutting of the flesh, cultic prostitution and practices of communication with the dead. Old Testament law was given to the nation of Israel, and although the Church has no duty to the Leviticus laws, there remain truths we can learn. All Scripture is given by inspiration of God, and is profitable for doctrine, for reproof, for correction, for instruction in righteousness (2 Timothy 3:16). So let's see what instruction and teachable truth we can glean that is profitable for Believers who have been gripped by the culture.

Under the New Covenant of Grace, prohibitions in a similar manner were expressed by Paul to the Church at Corinth encouraging the Corinthians believers to flee from rituals associated with demon worship. Consider this passage where he referenced the people of Israel.

1 Corinthians 10:18-22(NIV)

18Consider the people of Israel: Do not those who eat the sacrifices participate in the altar? 19 Do I mean then that food sacrificed to an idol is anything, or that an idol is anything? 20 No, but the sacrifices of pagans are offered to demons, not to God, and I do not want you to be participants with demons. 21 You cannot drink the cup of the Lord and the cup of demons too; you cannot have a part in both the Lord's table and the table of demons. 22 Are we trying to arouse the Lord's jealousy? Are we stronger than he?

The Apostle Paul is addressing some converts at Corinth, who took their freedom or liberty in grace too far. They understood that food offered to idols was nothing to them as they live in freedom under grace. They felt at liberty to partake at the meal tables that were offered to an idol and to partake at the table of the cup of the Lord's (Lord's Communion). The Apostle Paul set things in order by first affirming that neither the idol nor the food offered to them is nothing. He did not stop there but went on to address and to acknowledge that the "ritual practices" were offered to demons and not to the true and living God. He clearly recognized that the pagan rituals were demonic at its core and clearly states that he did not want the Church to participate with demons, prohibiting participation in all its rituals including its foods. The Scripture continues to say that the Church cannot have part in both, the table of the Lord and the table of demon practices. So the Law in Leviticus and the grace of the Church agrees on the same point relating to an idol or demonic worship. Since we are to glorify God in our bodies, it remains prudent that Believers refrain from any practices that shed blood, cuts and disfigures for superficial, casual or ritualistic pleasures.

Realizing that most people who cut, tattoo and body pierce do it for various reasons not associated with idol or demonic practices. However, many people have the names of their dead loved ones tattoo on their bodies as a form of memorial to the dead and religious symbols tattoos on their bodies as their statement to whom they worship. Gangs have certain emblems cut into their bodies and even on their faces to signify the numbers of murders performed in gang activity or deaths to their gang members. Some tattoo and pierce for decoration. Fraternities and Sororities also tattoo, cut and even burn symbols into their flesh signifying their love for their organization. A growing trend is tattooing, piercing and gauging of the body to levels of disfiguring and bizarreness and some pierce their tongues and other body parts for the participation of deviant activities. Some even go to the extreme of having surgical procedures done to disfigure their heads, add horns and divide their tongues like that of a snake. Teeth are sharpened and altered to mimic that of K-9 fangs and have their eyeball injected with colorful dyes. This stuff is from the spirits of darkness and these practices have slipped into the Church. One young man expressed that he was encouraged by a Pastor to gauge his earlobes. He had holes in his earlobes the size of a Florida lemon as he explained that Jesus Body was pierced so he felt closer to Jesus. Really?! Another person said her Pastor told her that piercing her body would help her win others to the Lord. Really?! Moreover, the list goes on! These extreme behaviors stem from unseen influences. It is profitable for the Church to understand that there may be things we participate in with the idea of liberty under grace, however its influence can be inimical when its sources are misunderstood. It seems good to honor the Lord with our bodies and stay away from these practices.

Now if you are a Believer and participating in piercings, tats, and even devil horns, my words to you are to stop it and participate no more. Turn from it and renew your mind with the Word of God and walk in the newness of the Spirit. The Holy Spirit will guide into all truth and uprightness with God the Father who is love. Perhaps you have done things to your body before you came to know the Lord, just know you are free. Be encouraged to walk in the grace that was delivered unto you when God saved you. Since Jesus saved you in your piercings, tats, and bodily altered state so live according to the new creation that you are in Christ. Let the Holy Spirit guide you in what to do concerning any altered ways.

Live from the wellspring of your spirit and not out of your lower fleshly nature. Here are some scriptures to consider:

Ephesians 2:1-22 (NIV)

2 As for you, you were dead in your transgressions and sins, ² in which you used to live when you followed the ways of this world and of the ruler of the kingdom of the air, the spirit who is now at work in those who are disobedient. ³ All of us also lived among them at one time, gratifying the cravings of our flesh[a] and following its desires and thoughts. Like the rest, we were by nature deserving of wrath. ⁴ But because of his great love for us, God, who is rich in mercy, ⁵ made us alive with Christ even when we were dead in transgressions— it is by grace you have been saved. ⁶ And God raised us up with Christ and seated us with him in the heavenly realms in Christ Jesus, ⁷ in order that in the coming ages he might show the incomparable riches of his grace, expressed in his kindness to us in Christ Jesus. ⁸ For it is by grace you have been saved, through faith—and this is not from yourselves, it is the gift of God— ⁹ not by works, so that no one can boast. ¹⁰ For we are God's handiwork, created in Christ Jesus to do good works, which God prepared in advance for us to do.¹¹ Therefore, remember that formerly you who are Gentiles by birth and called "uncircumcised" by those who call themselves "the circumcision" (which is done in the body by human hands)—¹² remember that at that time you were separate from Christ, excluded from *citizenship in Israel and foreigners to the covenants of the promise, without hope and without God in the world. ¹³ But now in Christ Jesus you who once were far away have been brought near by the blood of Christ.*

¹⁴ For he himself is our peace, who has made the two groups one and has destroyed the barrier, the dividing wall of hostility, ¹⁵ by setting aside in his flesh the law with its commands and regulations. His purpose was to create in himself one new humanity out of the two, thus making peace, ¹⁶ and in one body to reconcile both of them to God through the cross, by which he put to death their hostility. ¹⁷ He came and preached peace to you who were far away and peace to those who were near.¹⁸ For through him we both have access to the Father by one Spirit. ¹⁹ Consequently, you are no longer foreigners and strangers, but fellow citizens with God's people and also members of his household, ²⁰ built on the foundation of the apostles and prophets, with Christ Jesus himself as the chief cornerstone. ²¹ In him the whole building is joined together and rises to become a holy temple in the Lord. ²² And in him you too are being built together to become a dwelling in which God lives by his Spirit.

Ephesians 4:17-24 (NIV)

¹⁷So I tell you this, and insist on it in the Lord, that you must no longer live as the Gentiles do, in the futility of their thinking.¹⁸ They are darkened in their understanding and separated from the life of God because of the ignorance that is in them

due to the hardening of their hearts. [19] Having lost all sensitivity, they have given themselves over to sensuality so as to indulge in every kind of impurity, and they are full of greed. [20] That, however, is not the way of life you learned [21] when you heard about Christ and were taught in him in accordance with the truth that is in Jesus. [22] You were taught, with regard to your former way of life, to put off your old self, which is being corrupted by its deceitful desires; [23] to be made new in the attitude of your minds;[24] and to put on the new self, created to be like God in true righteousness and holiness.

Chapter 9

Church Discipline

"Cheap grace is the grace we bestow on ourselves. Cheap grace is the preaching of forgiveness without requiring repentance, baptism without church discipline, Communion without confession...Cheap grace is grace without discipleship, grace without the cross, grace without Jesus Christ, living and incarnate."

— Dietrich Bonhoeffer

Discipline in the Church

Tolerance and - "Don't Judge Me (DJM) "
Now let's talk about the issue concerning "tolerance" and "church discipline." It seems there is much tolerance going on in the Church and church discipline is almost non-existent. In a conversation with another Pastor, the subject of church discipline came up as we were discussing a disturbing matter going on in their church. "Does your church have a disciplinary

policy?" I asked. If so, "How is it implemented?" To my surprise the Pastor said, they are not in people's lives like that. They do not judge because Jesus said not to do it, and they leave all judgment to God. This answer was a clue perhaps as to why they were having the problems. They are gripped by the culture with what has become the escape goat clause for the world and now even the Church. That clause is "Don't Judge Me (DJM). " It is used to keep a person's wrong conduct from being addressed. They were not rightfully dividing the Word of God (2 Timothy 2:15); thus they had no policy for church discipline in place. Unfortunately in today's church world, most churches do not exercise church discipline even though the Apostle Paul give clear instruction on how to handle disruptions in the Church.

Rev. Kenneth E Hagin said that one can sometimes better understand something by looking at what it is not. So let's apply this thought and look at what church discipline is not. It is not to show someone their sin, not to be punitive, not to embarrass, ridicule or to humiliate, not to demean or to condemn in any way but to restore. Yes, that is right, To RESTORE! The entire principles of church discipline outlined by the Apostle Paul are for the restoration of the Believer. The lack of knowledge about this matter coupled with misguided emotions has caused the Church to shrink back and become tolerant of iniquitous conduct. The Church no long faces up to the unruly members in their local fellowships thus leaving the leaven to ferment the whole lump. Tolerance in the Church has taken on a new meaning from the pulpits to the pews with no corrective measures administered to lead to correction and restoration. Lack of discipline is unacceptable in the Body of Christ. Let's look at a biblical case for our guide.

1 Corinthians 5 The Message (MSG)

5 [1-2] I also received a report of scandalous sex within your church family, a kind that wouldn't be tolerated even outside the church: One of your men is sleeping with his stepmother. And you're so above it all that it doesn't even faze you! Shouldn't this break your hearts? Shouldn't it bring you to your knees in tears? Shouldn't this person and his conduct be confronted and dealt with?

[3-5] I'll tell you what I would do. Even though I'm not there in person, consider me right there with you, because I can fully see what's going on. I'm telling you that this is wrong. You must not simply look the other way and hope it goes away on its own. Bring it out in the open and deal with it in the authority of Jesus our Master. Assemble the community—I'll be present in spirit with you and our Master Jesus will be present in power. Hold this man's conduct up to public scrutiny. Let him defend it if he can! But if he can't, then out with him! It will be totally devastating to him, of course, and embarrassing to you. But better devastation and embarrassment

than damnation. You want him on his feet and forgiven before the Master on the Day of Judgment.

⁶⁻⁸ Your flip and callous arrogance in these things bothers me. You pass it off as a small thing, but it's anything but that. Yeast, too, is a "small thing," but it works its way through a whole batch of bread dough pretty fast. So get rid of this "yeast." Our true identity is flat and plain, not puffed up with the wrong kind of ingredient. The Messiah, our Passover Lamb, has already been sacrificed for the Passover meal, and we are the Unraised Bread part of the Feast. So let's live out our part in the Feast, not as raised bread swollen with the yeast of evil, but as flat bread—simple, genuine, unpretentious.

⁹⁻¹³ I wrote you in my earlier letter that you shouldn't make yourselves at home among the sexually promiscuous. I didn't mean that you should have nothing at all to do with outsiders of that sort. Or with crooks, whether blue- or white-collar. Or with spiritual phonies, for that matter. You'd have to leave the world entirely to do that! But I am saying that you shouldn't act as if everything is just fine when a friend who claims to be a Christian is promiscuous or crooked, is flip with God or rude to friends, gets drunk or becomes greedy and predatory. You can't just go along with this, treating it as acceptable behavior. I'm not responsible for what the outsiders do, but don't we have some responsibility for those within our community of believers? God decides on the outsiders, but we need

*to decide when our brothers and sisters are out of line
and, if necessary, clean house.*

Now follow the protocol. The nefarious behavior is
defined (sexual immorality), and the proper response
to how the Church should feel about such behavior
is given (ashamed, heartbroken to tears). The action
of discipline (called wrong, not overlooked, must
be confronted) and how it should be administered
(In the Authority of Jesus, before the Assembly) is
outlined. The indicted person's responsibility is to
give an account before the Assembly. This action
should produce a serious awareness of the sinful
behavior that should lead to repentance that is far
better than damnation before the Lord on the Day
of Judgment. The practice of sinful behavior by a
believing Christian is serious business as the Apostle
Paul makes clear here in 1 Corinthians 5:1-12. He
tells the Church at Corinth not the keep company with
those who are sexually immoral, and he also names a
few other things. He goes on to encourage the Church
in its responsibility to judge the unruly, flip and out of
line behaviors as unacceptable and if necessary expel
them from the local fellowship.

In mindset of Believers today, this sound harsh and
insensitive. Most Christians would ask, "What would
Jesus do (WWJD)"? Their answer would be, love
them and don't judge them. This is error and the best
scheme yet that Satan has ever pulled on the Church.

"Don't Judge Me" has always been the battle cry of the worldly culture. However, to the Church, it is polarizing and has a chilling effect on our assignment to call the sinner man to repent and to flee from the wrath of God which is to come. The Church armed with the Word of God is God's agent in the earth realm with the assignment to call men into life with Christ. In Matthew 7:1, Jesus did say, Judge not lest you be judged, but what did he mean? Does Paul contradict his Lord and Savior? The answer is No! The most common word for "judge" in the Greek Testament is the verb krino, found 114 times. It renders in English various terms, e.g., "judge," "determine," "condemn," "call in question," etc. The word means to "select"; to "distinguish"; then to "come to a conclusion of, make a determination". The basic meaning is neutral; only the context can tell whether is it used positively or negatively. The context of Matthew 7:1, Jesus was addressing the Pharisaic practices of judging. They determined that Jesus message of the Kingdom to be inadequate compared to the kind of Kingdom they anticipated and the kind of righteousness they were exhibiting. The only Kingdom and righteousness they knew was their own. Jesus was simply telling them not to judge Him by their standard because they did not know enough about God or his Kingdom. After all Jesus had come down from heaven to bring the good news of His Father's Kingdom. The Pharisees had no clue. The passage does not teach that judgments should never be made. Jesus makes this clear in

John 7:24, which says, Judge not according to the appearance, but judge righteous judgment. Here Jesus is encouraging righteous judgment. Is Jesus confused? No! Neither is Paul in contradiction with Jesus in his judgment in the Church at Corinth. Thus clearly judgments are sometimes needed, those making the distinctions should be certain not to do it through their self-righteousness. Consider these Scriptures to the Church.

Romans 3:4 (NIV)

⁴ Not at all! Let God be true, and every human being a liar. As it is written: "So that you may be proved right when you speak and prevail when you judge."

1 Corinthians 5:12 (NIV)

¹² What business is it of mine to judge those outside the church? Are you not to judge those inside?

Galatians 2:11 (KJV)

¹¹ But when Peter was come to Antioch, I withstood him to the face, because he was to be blamed.

Forgiveness for the Offender

Now let's continue with Church Discipline. The Apostle Paul gives more instruction in His second letter to the Church at Corinth; concerning the forgiveness and restoration of the offender.

2 Corinthians 2:5-8 The Message (MSG)

5-8 Now, regarding the one who started all this—the person in question who caused all this pain—I want you to know that I am not the one injured in this as much as, with a few exceptions, all of you. So I don't want to come down too hard. What the majority of you agreed to as punishment is punishment enough. Now is the time to forgive this man and help him back on his feet. If all you do is pour on the guilt, you could very well drown him in it. My counsel now is to pour on the love.

9-11 The focus of my letter wasn't on punishing the offender but on getting you to take responsibility for the health of the church. So if you forgive him, I forgive him. Don't think I'm carrying around a list of personal grudges. The fact is that I'm joining in with your forgiveness, as Christ is with us, guiding us. After all, we don't want to unwittingly give Satan an opening for yet more mischief—we're not oblivious to his sly ways!

Again let's follow the protocol. The Apostle Paul makes clear the purpose of the discipline that was not to punish the offender, but that the Church would take responsibility for it health and to call the offender to repentance. He recalls the offender (the one who caused the pain) to the Assembly that administered the punishment. He encourages mercy and the extension of forgiveness (not to come down to hard, pour on no more guilt). He encouraged them to begin a process of restoration to restore him (help him back on his feet,) with love to close the door of Satan over his life. In this next passage of Scripture, Paul describes the outcome of the discipline. It worked repentance, righteousness, a pure heart and a deeper tie with God.

2 Corinthians 7:8-13 The Message (MSG)

[8-9] *I know I distressed you greatly with my letter. Although I felt awful at the time, I don't feel at all bad now that I see how it turned out. The letter upset you, but only for a while. Now I'm glad—not that you were upset, but that you were jarred into turning things around. You let the distress bring you to God, not drive you from him. The result was all gain, no loss.*

[10] *Distress that drives us to God does that. It turns us around. It gets us back in the way of salvation. We never regret that kind of pain. But those who let distress drive them away from God are full of regrets, end up on a deathbed of regrets.*

[11-13] *And now, isn't it wonderful all the ways in which this distress has goaded you closer to God? You're more alive, more concerned, more sensitive, more reverent, more human, more passionate, more responsible. Looked at from any angle, you've come out of this with purity of heart. And that is what I was hoping for in the first place when I wrote the letter. My primary concern was not for the one who did the wrong or even the one*

wronged, but for you—that you would realize and act upon the deep, deep ties between us before God. That's what happened—and we felt just great.

Hebrews 12:4-11 (NIV)

⁴ In your struggle against sin, you have not yet resisted to the point of shedding your blood. ⁵ And have you completely forgotten this word of encouragement that addresses you as a father addresses his son? It says,

*"My son, do not make light of the Lord's discipline,
    and do not lose heart when he rebukes you,
⁶ because the Lord disciplines the one he loves,
    and he chastens everyone he accepts as his son."[a]*

⁷ Endure hardship as discipline; God is treating you as his children. For what children are not disciplined by their father?⁸ If you are not disciplined—and everyone undergoes discipline—then you are not legitimate, not true sons and daughters at all.⁹ Moreover, we have all had human fathers who disciplined us and we respected them for it. How much more should we submit to the Father of spirits and live! ¹⁰ They disciplined us for a little while as they thought best; but God disciplines us for our good, in order that we may share in his holiness. ¹¹ No discipline seems pleasant at the time, but painful. Later on, however, it produces a harvest of righteousness and peace for those who have been trained by it.

Let's observe the results of the discipline. Paul states that it was painful for him to have to write the letter. As a matter of fact, he felt awful for a little while but was glad he did so because of the fruit the disciplined produced. It caused them to turn things around (repentance). These feelings are true for all Pastors and even parents. It is not pleasant for the moment to have to discipline, but necessary to do so. The correction brought them to God and did not drive them from God; the results were all gain. NO LOSS! Oh boy, is this contrary to Church culture and even in families today. Most people think that correction drives people away. Paul goes on to say that those who let the correction drive them away from God end up on a junk heap of regrets. However, he rejoiced in knowing that the correction made the Church more alive, more concerned, more sensitive, more reverent, more human, more passionate, more responsible with purity of heart. The purpose and end goal of the correction is that the Church as a whole would recognize and act upon the deep ties between the Believer before God. In the letter to the Hebrew Christians, Paul reiterate the same principles. Encouraging them not to make light of the Lord's discipline and lose heart when he rebukes, because the Lord is a perfect and good Father, who loves perfectly. He loves those whom he corrects. He said to endure the hardship of discipline for it produces a harvest of righteousness and peace to who are trained by it.

When it comes to church or parental discipline, it is best received when discussed in peace times. Pastors should minister principles of Church discipline in times of peace and when joy is flowing in a congregation.

Please realize that all unruly behaviors will not merit open discipline. Some people who are challenged will most often be dealt with privately, and that will be all that is needed. Some will hear a message that will convince of sin and get it right. There are some with unrepentant open sin who will have to be dealt with openly even as Paul did in Corinth. Here's an example.

Pregnant Not Married
Here are two ladies with similar stories but with very different endings. Both are Believers in Christ and were pregnant out to wedlock. The first young lady advised the Pastor of her pregnancy, and he reached out to the young man involved because he was not a church member or a Believer. He was neither receptive nor a responsible young man. To her credit, she did not run from her responsibility as a church member. Although she understood and appeared to accept the discipline outlined by the standards of the local church body and the Word, she had a major protest going on within her heart. She did not believe she had done anything dishonoring by being pregnant. Now let's look at this.

In one sense of the word, she was correct. Think about it, the Bible does not say flee pregnancy, it says flee fornication. The Church has often gotten this wrong and has far too long focused on the result of the issue at heart rather than the issue. Pregnancy, provided that all things be equal, is inevitable when a man and woman come together sexually; the natural order of things. However, the biblical context for pregnancy is within the bonds of marriage. This young lady did not get this and would not accept this. The culture gripped her. She thought the whole thing was about the pregnancy, rather than the lifestyle of fornication that is prohibited in Scripture for the Believer. She would not accept the Word of God, on the issue. Her attitude became flipped, and cavalier and the Sunday worship atmosphere was vexed as she stood before God's people. She left that Sunday, convinced she had been mistreated and managed somehow to convince others of this idea also. She moves away chasing the young man and never really worshiped the Lord wholeheartedly. Her results were heartbreak, and abandonment by the young man, financially ruined with undisciplined children.

Now the second young lady, however, called for repentance out of respect for the Pastor. She immediately asked for forgiveness for dishonoring the Lord by her behavior. She explained she had gotten away from the fellowship by allowing other things to distract her. She was dealing with loneliness when an old flame had returned home from college, and they started spending much time together. He was not a member of a local church fellowship. She further explained she had rekindled this relationship and got emotionally involved, and it became physically intimate very quickly. She acknowledged the Word and made no excuses for what happened. She took responsibility as a Believer before God. She asked God and the Pastor to forgive her and now she wanted her local fellowship family to forgive her and to pray for her. She asked the Pastor to stand with her as she addressed the local family body. Her prayer request was for strength against the pressure to abort the child. She would not compound the problem by aborting the child. She solicited the prayers of the Saints that availed much. She spoke very clearly, and humbly and graciously from her heart. Afterward prayer was made for her, and communion was administered. The anointing was very strong, and there was not a dry eye in the worship service. There was such a sweet Spirit in the atmosphere because all could clearly see the love of God demonstrated through forgiveness and power. This young lady married the baby's Father and moved to Washington D.C. Throughout her pregnancy, God provided everything she needed for the baby. She is prospering in her marriage, and they both are serving the Lord.

The Lord allows us to learn and see discipline as healthy and wholesome for the Church. If we would allow this teaching of God's Word to work in the Church, we will see the reverence and respect for God and His Word return to the Church with power. Lord help us to get there!

As we look to the soon appearing of our Lord, we must continue in sound doctrine, and free ourselves from the snare of cultural trends that have gripped the Church. We must return Church discipline back into the church. Then and only then will we see the reverence return to the praise and glory of God. Grace will be more evident in the life of the Believer because we will have aligned ourselves with the biblical grace that is prescribed in Scripture. Take this thought to mind!

"The community of the saints is not an "ideal" community consisting of perfect and sinless men and women, where there is no need of further repentance. No, it is a community which proves that it is worthy of the gospel of forgiveness by constantly and sincerely proclaiming *God's* forgiveness...Sanctification means driving out the world from the Church as well as separating the Church from the world. But the purpose of such discipline is not to establish a community of the perfect, but a community consisting of men who really live under the forgiving mercy of God."
— Dietrich Bonhoeffer, *The Cost of Discipleship*

1 John 3:9-10The Message (MSG)

9-10 People conceived and brought into life by God don't make a practice of sin. How could they? God's seed is deep within them, making them who they are. It's not in the nature of the God-begotten to practice and parade sin. Here's how you tell the difference between God's children and the Devil's children: The one who won't practice righteous ways isn't from God, nor is the one who won't love brother or sister. A simple test.

Chapter 10

Church and the Hollywood Culture

"Example is not the main thing in influencing others. It is the only thing."

— *Albert Schweitzer*

Cultural Christianity at its best is most recently revealed in Hollywood "Reality TV" with Pastors. Reality television is a genre of television programming that documents unscripted real-life situations with a focus on drama and personal conflict; unlike a documentary that seeks to educate viewers about a particular issue. Let's keep it "real" is the idea. The insatiable appetite that craves drama and personal conflict in the lives of others is another all time curiosity in American culture. For some, the dirtier it is, the better it is. Popular reality shows like, The Real Housewives, Teen Moms, The Apprentice, Jersey Shores, and the Bachelor are programs that interest viewers because in some way they can relate.

Like anything else, not all Reality TV is bad. Some are fascinating and promote wholesome values. Interestingly enough, Reality TV has crossed over into the Church, opening up the reality world of some Pastors and their families. Reality Preachers can be tricky because Hollywood does not have a Biblical Worldview and tends to paint the Church through the eyes of secularism to validate their worldview. I do not say this genre of television programming cannot be useful for the propagation of the Gospel. However, its use so far has at best promoted the carnal (fleshly) nature and the idea of "Hollywood Preachers" who suggest that money, cars, and houses draw people to Jesus Christ. It is Gospel-lite at its best. The idea that the un-Believer will come to Jesus as the result of seeing "the blessings" (money, cars, houses) of the Lord is bogus and not biblical according to New Testament teaching. Here is the Word of God on how people will come to know Christ.

1 Corinthians 1:20-22 King James Version (KJV)

[20] *Where is the wise? Where is the scribe? Where is the disputer of this world? hath not God made foolish the wisdom of this world?*

[21] *For after that in the wisdom of God the world by wisdom knew not God,* **it pleased God by the foolishness of preaching to save them that believe.**

[22] *For the Jews require a sign, and the Greeks seek after wisdom:*

Romans 10:14-16 King James Version (KJV)

*14 How then shall they call on him in whom they have not believed? And how shall they believe in him of whom they have not heard? and **how shall they hear without a preacher?***

15 And how shall they preach, except they be sent? as it is written, How beautiful are the feet of them that preach the gospel of peace, and bring glad tidings of good things!

16 But they have not all obeyed the gospel. For Esaias saith, Lord, who hath believed our report?

It is clear that God ordained the tool of preaching, as foolish as it may be, as the means by which men are to hear about Jesus Christ to be saved. It is not by seeing or having "earthly goods" God has blessed his people with that causes men to be saved or to desire to be saved! This idea often leads to false conversions and mental assent to Christ. In the Scriptures, many people followed Jesus for various reasons during his earthly ministry. There were great multitudes that followed him as long as he was feeding them but when Jesus spoke of the true meat of what it meant to follow him, they left him. They did not want to take up a cross daily to follow him. They did not want to drink of His blood nor eat of His flesh. These were hard saying; they could not bear it!

Ministers of the Gospel should be dignified and strive to live about reproach. The late Dr. Edwin Louis Cole would encourage men to guard, guide and govern their families well; fulfill their duty to direct, correct and protect, nourish, cherish, and admonish their families. This behavior should then overflow into the service and assignments of God as an example for others to witness. In first Timothy, the Apostle Paul outlines qualifications for Leaders and anyone who desires to be a Leader in the Church.

1 Timothy 3:1-7 New International Version (NIV)

3 Here is a trustworthy saying: Whoever aspires to be an overseer desires a noble task. ² Now the overseer is to be above reproach, faithful to his wife, temperate, self-controlled, respectable, hospitable, able to teach, ³ not given to drunkenness, not violent but gentle, not quarrelsome, not a lover of money. ⁴ He must manage his own family well and see that his children obey him, and he must do so in a manner worthy of full respect. ⁵ (If anyone does not know how to manage his own family, how can he take care of God's church?) ⁶ He must not be a recent convert, or he may become conceited and fall under the same judgment as the devil.⁷ He must also have a good reputation with outsiders so that he will not fall into disgrace and into the devil's trap.

This passage of Scripture gives a great example of what a Christian Leader's conduct ought to be! Church

Leaders should reconsider their participation in the mayhem of a Gospel-lite message and give deeper thought before exposing themselves and their family to the worldliness of pop-culture. Ministers and their families are targets of unwanted scrutiny and Reality TV adds to the unwanted examinations.

Renewing the Mind

"As with every aspect of our sanctification, the renewal of the mind may be painful and difficult. It requires hard work and discipline, inspired by a sacrificial love for Christ and a burning desire to build up His body, the Church. Developing a Christian worldview means submitting our entire self to God, in an act of devotion and service to Him."
— Nancy Pearcey, *Total Truth: Liberating Christianity from its Cultural Captivity*

As we await the coming of the Lord, the true Believers light will shine brighter as the world becomes darker. The Church assignment has not changed. We are to be salt and light! Salt seasons and light dispels darkness. Every Believer must let their light shine (Matthew 5:13-16) in this season. It is my hope that readers of "Gripped by the Culture" have received some insightful information on trends and common behaviors that are contrary to Scripture. It is my prayer that every reader will take an inventory of their life as a member of the Body of Christ and make a conscience decision to align with the Word of God.

For spiritual enrichment and edification, meditate on the Word of God each day. Daily meditations on Scripture coupled with corresponding actions will renew the mind, bringing the will and the emotions into the obedience of the Word of God. If the culture has gripped you, find out what God has to say about your situation and claim the promises of that Word by faith. You will break free as you renew your mind and God will make an end of it in your life.

Ephesians 4:21-24 (NIV)

[21] *When you heard about Christ and were taught in him in accordance with the truth that is in Jesus.*[22] *You were taught, with regard to your former way of life, to put off your old self, which is being corrupted by its deceitful desires;* [23] *to be made new in the attitude of your minds;* [24] *and to put on the new self, created to be like God in true righteousness and holiness.*

Romans 12:1-3 (NIV)

[12] *Therefore, I urge you, brothers and sisters, in view of God's mercy, to offer your bodies as a living sacrifice, holy and pleasing to God—this is your true and proper worship.* [2] *Do not conform to the pattern of this world, but be transformed by the renewing of your mind. Then you will be able to test and approve what God's will is—his good, pleasing and perfect will.*

Colossians 3:9-10 (NIV)

[9] Do not lie to each other, since you have taken off your old self with its practices [10] and have put on the new self, which is being renewed in knowledge in the image of its Creator.

Remember! The Bible is the most relevant book of all ages! It is never obsolete, and its truths endure to all generations. Thus it is the trusted source for inspiration from God, and is profitable for doctrine, for reproof, for correction, for instruction in righteousness. This book canvasses common cultural influences in the Church and will shine light from the Scriptures for transformation for those who are "Gripped by the Culture."

My prayer for you!

Father in Jesus Name,

I pray that the God of our Lord Jesus Christ, the glorious Father, may give you the Spirit of wisdom and revelation, so that you may know him better. I pray that the eyes of your heart may be enlightened in order that you may know the hope to which he has called you, the riches of his glorious inheritance in his holy people, and his incomparably great power for us who believe. That power is the same as the mighty strength he exerted when he raised Christ from the dead and seated him at his right hand in the heavenly realms, far above all rule and authority, power and dominion, and every name that is invoked, not only in the present age but also in the one to come. And God placed all things under his feet and appointed him to be head over everything for the church, which is his body, the fullness of him who fills everything in every way.

I pray that out of his glorious riches he may strengthen you with power through his Spirit in your inner being, so that Christ may dwell in your hearts through faith. And I pray that you, being rooted and established in love, may have power, together with all the Lord's holy people, to grasp how wide and long and high and deep is the love of Christ, and to know this love that surpasses knowledge—that you may be filled to the measure of all the fullness of God. I pray that your love may abound more and more in knowledge and depth of insight, so that you may be able to discern what is best and may be pure and blameless for the day of Christ, filled with the fruit of righteousness that comes through Jesus Christ—to the glory and praise of God. I continually ask God to fill you with the knowledge of his will through all the wisdom and understanding that the Spirit gives, so that you may live a life worthy of the Lord and please him in every way: bearing fruit in every good work, growing in the knowledge of God, being strengthened with all power according to his glorious might so that you may have great endurance and patience, and giving joyful thanks to the Father, who has qualified you to share in the inheritance of his holy people in the kingdom of light. For he has rescued us from the dominion of darkness and brought us into the kingdom of the Son he loves, in whom we have redemption, the forgiveness of sins. I pray this so that the name of our Lord Jesus may be glorified in you, and you in him, according to the grace of our God and the Lord Jesus Christ.

AMEN!!!

Contact

Ericka McCrutcheon
Joint Heirs Fellowship Church
P.O Box 750153
Houston, TX 77275-0153
Ph: (281) 922-0901